# ECONOMICS FOR EVERYONE

Keith Norris studied economics at Bristol University and University College, London. He is Reader in Economics at Brunel University and has acted as economic adviser in several official organisations including the Pay Board and the Royal Commission on the Distribution of Income and Wealth.

Lord Vaizey is Professor of Economics and Head of the School of Social Sciences, Brunel University. He was previously Fellow and Tutor of Worcester College, Oxford and Fellow of St Catherine's College, Cambridge. He is a consultant to the UN and OECD and is a frequent broadcaster and writer on economic problems. He contributes regular articles to the *Times Higher Educational Supplement*, the *Times Educational Supplement*, *Listener* and *Spectator* and has written several books including *The Economics of Education*, *Education in the Modern World*, *The Sleepless Lunch*, and *Social Democracy*.

The authors have collaborated before in writing *The Political Economy of Education* (1972) and *The Economics of Research and Technology* (1973).

TEACH YOURSELF BOOKS

# ECONOMICS FOR EVERYONE

**Keith Norris and John Vaizey**

TEACH YOURSELF BOOKS
Hodder and Stoughton

*First Impression 1977*



ISBN 0 340 21905 X

*Printed and bound in Great Britain for Hodder and Stoughton Paperbacks, a division of Hodder and Stoughton Ltd, Mill Road, Dunton Green, Sevenoaks, Kent, (Editorial Office; 47 Bedford Square, London WC1 3DP) by Richard Clay (The Chaucer Press) Ltd., Bungay, Suffolk*

# Contents

# Introduction

Economics is a subject that changes as events change, and develops as economists develop their interests. This book is a progress report for the intelligent layman on the recent and present state of the subject, with special reference to the UK economy. It concentrates, first of all, on the developed economies. The problems of extremely poor countries, as Gunnar Myrdal's *Asian Drama* so brilliantly indicates, are very different from those of an advanced industrial country. So, too, are those of an economy where extremely rapid technical and social change is occurring, as in Spain or Brazil. In concentrating on Britain, we are studying an economy which resembles a whole family of western industrialised economies.

The book starts with three chapters which are concerned with macro-economics, or the economics of any economy as a whole. Chapter 1 defines economics as an area of study. Chapter 2 introduces some analysis which is fundamental to a thorough understanding of how the economy as a whole operates.

The major recent economic problem has been inflation. It has assailed the whole western world in an exaggerated form since the mid 1960s, and it raises difficult issues of description, analysis and prescription. These are the subject of a whole chapter, Chapter 3. These two chapters lead on to a consideration, in Chapter 4, of the way governments and governmental-type bodies seek to manage the economy. They have multiple objectives—full employment, no inflation, high government expenditure and low taxation rates—which are to a greater or lesser extent incompatible. One of the major problems both in theory and in practice is to delimit government policies so that they do not make the situation worse and hopefully make it better. In Britain, over a thirty-year span, there has been so great a variety of experience with different policies that there is a wealth of evidence that may be brought to bear on what it is necessary, possible, desirable (and the reverse in all these cases) for governments to do.

The book then examines several sectors of the economy at a less aggregative level. One is the competitive sector, considered in Chapter 5, of small businesses, and of commodities and services where consumers are basically the decision-makers as to what shall be produced. It is in this chapter that the basic concepts of supply and demand are explained. Chapter 6 is on large firms, including the multinationals, who control a large part of the economy. Chapter 7 looks at the public sector and at state activities like health care and education, where control is exercised ultimately by Parliament.

The basic question of who is paid what is dealt with in Chapter 8, which leads on to a discussion of what determines the distribution of income between people and between classes, and how public actions, both of expenditure and of taxation, affect this distribution.

The British economy operates to an extraordinary degree in an international context, since about one third of the country's needs are imported and paid for by exports, and Britain is party to many international economic agreements which circumscribe and in some circumstances prescribe its own activities. Chapter 9 raises these vital questions of international trade and payments.

The book ends with an attempt (Chapter 10) to describe the main kinds of economy in the world, seeking to show that the British, or western industrial, way of economic life is but one of many possible ways of life. Perhaps by the end of the book some idea of the complexity of economic life, and the extreme difficulty of attempting to understand it, will have been given to the reader.

The books for further reading have been grouped according to the subject matter of each of the ten chapters, although some books will cover several chapters. In general they are restricted to those available in paperback form.

# I

# What Economics is about

## The problems that economists tackle

Economics is a subject that grew out of political economy. Adam Smith, who wrote *The Wealth of Nations* in 1776, defined the scope of economics as just that—what it was that caused nations to grow wealthy, and what policies statesmen should adopt in order to ensure that their country grew rich. Writing before the French Revolution, but at the beginning of the American War of Independence, Adam Smith, who was Professor of Moral Philosophy at Glasgow, argued against arbitrary and wasteful aristocratic government, and in favour of leaving businessmen and traders free to pursue their own interests. The great utilitarian philosophers, like Bentham and Mill, built on this foundation—first, that each man could alone know his own best interest, and, further, that the sum of everybody pursuing his own interest was the greatest good of the greatest number. This was the basis of the nineteenth-century doctrine of *laissez-faire*—'let do'—in which the state was given a minimal economic role.

Economics as it developed became the science of business decisions. Alfred Marshall, 1842–1924, probably the greatest English economist, described economics as the study of mankind in the ordinary business of life. This did not exclude study of some questions of state activity—for example, old age pensions and unemployment insurance—but it focused the attention of economists on what businessmen did. But as the twentieth century progressed, a series of pressing problems rapidly developed which went far outside the scope of the study of business. Unemployment, inflation and war, have all been major twentieth-century phenomena, and economists have had to learn to deal with them. Lord Robbins defined the subject just before the great slump of the early 1930s as the study of the problem of allocating scarce resources among alternative ends. This recognises one important truth—that economists are often concerned with the relative cost of two or more possible means of achieving a given objective, such as should the Channel be crossed by ships, by a bridge, or by a tunnel—but it ignores another truth, that economists are often concerned with the problem of providing work for the unemployed. Lord Keynes, 1883–1946, the polymath who solved the problem of how to control unemployment, probably came nearest the mark when he discussed the subject of economics as being not so much a set of blueprints, or of settled answers to specific questions, but as more like a toolbox, where people took out particular tools (or habits of thought) to tackle particular problems as they came up.

Most economists are trained by fairly similar university and college courses which introduce such notions as supply and demand, the market and prices, and the elements in the social scene that determine the total flow of goods and services and the level of prices. Economists comment on the movements of prices and on international trade.

A practical, positivistic way of approaching economics is to look at what economists actually do. In the USSR and other socialist countries they are taught the Marxist tools, notably that the political and social superstructure of society is changed by the alteration of the economic basis of society, and that the economic basis alters the relative position of different classes in society. Capitalism represents the era of the triumph of businessmen; it is succeeded by socialism, when the workers are in control. But in practice Marxist economists in the USSR are concerned chiefly with planning the flow of raw material and labour into various capital and consumer goods, and with determining the final mix of goods and services made available to the population.

Outside the USSR, many economists, especially in the Third World, work for the government doing essentially similar tasks. In India, for example, the Planning Commission is staffed by economists who draw up programmes for investment in agriculture, energy and transport, and allocate government expenditure between education and rural development. In the advanced industrial countries government economists may be employed in examining the details of public programmes—for example, calculating the likely pattern of demand for transport, or for health care—or they may be advising on the policies which Parliament has to adopt to avoid inflation and unemployment, and to achieve economic growth without falling into a substantial deficit with foreign countries. Economists working for business try to forecast the demand for, say, textiles, or electronic equipment, and to second-guess what the government economists are recommending.

## Economics and other disciplines

We see, then, that economists are mainly concerne[illegible] —that is to say, who works in what line of country—w[illegible] or will be produced, at what price and in what quantities a product will sell, what is the right sort of banking policy to adopt, what is the proper level and mix of taxation. They advise government departments, firms, stockholders, and they write in the business sections of newspapers. Many politicians have been trained fully or partially as economists and the subject has once more become a consideration of the proper level and direction of state action. It embraces those who say there should be much more state intervention and those who say that there should be much less. A common and true accusation against economists is that they are 'materialistic'. It is obvious from the jobs that they do that this is in fact an accurate depiction of their art (or science). But as economics has grown to its present size as a discipline, with many thousands of acolytes, other disciplines have grown up alongside it. The difference between these and economics lies partly in their methods and partly in what they study. Many questions in human life, however, spread right across these conventional barriers.

A good example is the changing role of women in contemporary society. Women have always had jobs—in the fields, or in the cotton mills of early nineteenth-century England, and recently as secretaries, doctors and factory workers. But most 'women's work', housekeeping and child-rearing, has not been done for payment; it has been accepted as part of the business of being a wife, and it has not been the subject of study by economists. If the work had been done for payment—if every wife had gone next door to work and been paid by the next-door neighbour—then it would have been 'economic'. In fact, however, the study of women's work has been a matter for sociologists, and the differences between male and female attitudes to the home have been studied by psychologists. Sociologists study society as a whole. Their basic books have been those of Marx and Durkheim, and their aim has been to [illegible]d general laws that determine the working of society.

[illegible]Marx is, however, also claimed by the economists. The [illegible]erence between the sociologists and economists has been [illegible] the 'economic' aspects of society have largely been left on [illegible] side by sociologists, while the economists have tended to take as given such matters as family structure, attitudes to work, and to the consumption of goods and services, and the relative status of sexes and of races. But when an issue like the changing status of women comes up, then the barriers between sociology and economics are blurred. Should women get equal pay? And what will be the consequences of their doing so? What would be the implications of different arrangements for child care so that men have to assume far more responsibility than they have in the past? All these matters straddle the boundaries of economics and sociology. So, too, do matters concerned with trade unions and industrial relations, where the economic consequences of particular methods of wage determination shade easily into what have traditionally been thought of as the sociological; the need, for instance, for people to think of themselves as part of a group and to gain their self-esteem mainly from the opinions of those with whom they are in daily contact, so that a trade union may often take a course of action that makes members' incomes lower than they might otherwise be, for reasons that are (to an economist) apparently 'irrational'.

There is a tendency in economics to identify 'rational' behaviour with that course of action that leads to monetary gain and eschews loss; and a tendency to refer to the most important elements in a situation (like trade union loyalty) as 'institutional'—a word derived from Thorstein Veblen's work, and meaning a social arrangement, or attitude, that is determined outside the economic sphere.

The problem of the jurisdiction of different subjects is now most acute in the case of politics. Since the state has become all powerful in the USSR and its associated countries, and since it has become dominant elsewhere, most economists advise governments, or analyse the behaviour of governments. When politicians act, are they acting as economic or political agents? There is a body of knowledge, the subject of the academic study of politics, which is concerned directly with political institutions and behaviour. In many respects this behaviour and these institutions are also economic. It is for this sort of reason that it has been argued that the nature and methods of economics have become deeply tainted by politics. Indeed, in some circles, the idea of an 'economist' is of a deeply committed socialist, while to many socialists economists are businessmen's lackeys.

## The methodology of economics

The methodology of economics is, therefore, not as simple as it seems. In China, Russia, America and Spain a physicist would set about tackling a problem in essentially the same way, though he might begin his day with an ode to Mao, or to Lenin, or by going to church, depending on where he finds himself. How does an economist work? Essentially, most economists are desk-bound. It is desirable that a man or woman who writes about the economics of agriculture should know at first hand about crops and herds, but all too often that is not the case. For an economist's data are statistics. These statistics concern measures of the total volume of production of various commodities; the numbers of people employed; the volumes of sales; the total amounts of payments; index numbers of price changes, of the changes of the amount of money in circulation, and of credit extended by banks and other loan institutions. Some of these data are collected by private bodies, notably trade associations, banks and trade unions, but the great bulk of statistics are collected by the government and its agencies. Until recently in the UK, the statistics were collected by government in its ordinary business of life. Because cars are licensed annually for taxation, it was easy to say how many cars were on the road. As bicycles were not taxed, the numbers on the road had to be guessed or inferred. More recently, however, citizens in the five-yearly census, and businesses more frequently, have been required to fill in forms which yield data that will be of use to economists, ranging from their incomes to their expenditure habits. These data are collected and processed and, when published, are available for economists to manipulate.

To these are added the results of market surveys undertaken by various business organisations which yield information on consumer behaviour—knowing who watches the television and when, for example, is important for people who are selling alternative forms of leisure activities.

Having access to all these data, which can be fed into computers, or calculated on smaller machines, an economist will set out to answer a range of questions by a set of fairly standard techniques. If he is interested in the movement of the economy as a whole, he will take all production, aggregate it under various heads, notably capital goods (plant, machinery and building), consumer durables (cars, furniture, electrical equipment for the home), and consumption goods (food, leisure expenditure). He will set out the various channels—exports, government, local government, the nationalised industries and private firms—by which the production is directed into the hands (and mouths) of consumers. He will set out the various steps that need to be taken to boost production or cut consumption so that they both balance.

One of his major problems will be to try to convert *money* figures into *real* figures. Most of the data presented to the economist are in terms of money and are affected by changes in the level of prices, whereas he is usually interested in the quantity of physical goods and services. It is essential in economics to grasp the distinction between real and money magnitudes and why it is the former that is usually the most important. Most of us are painfully aware that we are no better off if our incomes increase by 10% while prices increase at the same rate. That is, while our money incomes go up by 10% our real incomes are unchanged—the quantity of goods and services we can buy remains the same. We shall come across this distinction several times in this book.

The data available on retail sectors may be further broken down to fit consumers into their particular socio-economic group. This is largely the sphere of micro-economics, which has traditionally been built around the behaviour of individual consumers, workers and firms. A key concept here is *elasticity*, relying upon the differential calculus, or the consequences upon one thing of very small changes in a related activity. Thus, as incomes rise, people tend to buy more of the more expensive commodities like luxury foods. How much extra they buy, for each additional unit of income, is the income elasticity of demand for that product.

A growing number of problems involving the manipulation of very large quantities of data are now manageable by computer, and computerised models of the economy are rapidly altering our conception of how it works. Does this have any effect upon what economists think about?

## Economics and political economy

There are those who would argue that as a result of the work of a number of Austrian thinkers, notably Menger, 1840–1921, a general system of economic reasoning has been established which is valid for all time for all societies. The argument is that there are certain axioms about human behaviour—such as that man is a maximising creature—which, if followed through logically, give a general model of an economy where, on certain assumptions, the allocation of resources is optimal—that is, it cannot be 'bettered', because any alterations imposed by any agency such as the state would leave more people even worse off than it would other people better off. It has been hotly argued by supporters of this school of thought that this is the case.

The opposition is mounted on three grounds: first, that the general model is fallacious and contains self-contradictory elements, notably that it does not allow for the effects of the passage of time upon the mutual interaction of elements of the model; second, that the true picture of events is that economic activity is contingent upon historical circumstance and happenchance, and that the idea of a 'general' science of economics is absurd and unhistorical; and third, that in practice, the 'general equilibrium economists' always commend a course of action which is pro-*laissez-faire* and anti-government intervention. This, it is argued, is itself strong evidence that 'economics' as a 'science' is in fact an ideology.

But in reply the economists of this persuasion would maintain that their method of analysis is 'positivistic'—that is to say, 'positive' economics begins with given data, and then applies a body of general economic reasoning to it. This body of doctrine generally teaches that market solutions are best—for example, that if there is a shortage of petrol, the best way of dealing with it is by raising the price rather than by rationing—but this is not because of any particular ideology, but rather because the world is in fact thus made. With respect to any political or social presuppositions they are completely neutral. Who owns what, or who gets what—that is, the purpose of economic activity—is not their concern. As technicians they are interested in the techniques of economic activity. They may be fanatical Hindus or Communists in their private lives, but professionally they are as neutral as any dentist is when she looks into somebody's mouth and decides whether or not dental disease is present. As a scientist, a dentist is not interested in whether the patient is a mass-murderer or Gandhi, or whether he is a cannibal or a vegetarian, except in so far as it affects his dental hygiene. Thus, an economic scientist would say that the USSR is extremely inefficient in the way that it distributes consumers' goods and services; but this is a clinical, nor a moral, judgement about Soviet communism.

Another tradition in economic science harks back to Adam Smith, 1723–90, Ricardo, 1772–1823 and Marx, 1818–83 and is associated with Gunnar Myrdal, 1898– , the Swedish economist. It maintains that there is a radical difference between the economist and the physical scientist because the economist cannot be neutral in the affairs that he discusses. His claim to scientific objectivity is really a claim to intellectual honesty; it is a requirement that he should state his value assumptions as clearly as possible, and search his heart for the values that are so deep that he is unaware that he holds them. This is the tradition of political economy. In many respects there is no difference in practice between economics and political economy; set the same problem, followers of the two schools will come up with the same sort of answer and will be able to engage in dialogue. But there tends to be a difference between the sort of questions that economists and political economists find interesting: economists are more interested in prices, and what causes markets to behave as they do, while political economists are more interested in governments, trade unions and organisations. Political economists do not regard it as improper to consider questions that economists claim they leave to sociologists or students of politics.

In this book we have tended to concentrate on the questions that practising economists deal with. This is, in a sense, an amalgamation of the traditions of 'positive' economics and of political economy, for the questions tend to be those of political economy, while the actual techniques are often those adopted by 'positive' economists. But it will be made plain throughout what (so far as we know) our value premises are, and the sorts of prejudices that you should look out for.

## The various sorts of economies

One of the problems of economics is that many different sorts of economies exist. If we go through the world at present we can classify them in several different sorts of ways. One is by their relative degree of richness—measured perhaps by the amount of energy used per head of population. That in turn is an indication of the kind of technology that they use. In 1973, for example, at one extreme were the United States, Canada and Sweden, which used over a hundred times as much energy per person as most of the African states, about sixty times as much as India, and twice as much as the countries of Western Europe. This is some sort of indication of the fact that these three countries have economies that are based upon advanced industrial technology, that they have big sectors of manufacturing industry, complex 'service' sectors—including education and health—and that they have exploited rich natural resources, while in Africa the agriculture is for the most part primitive, and industry is largely hand craft.

Another way of classifying economies is by the way in which economic decisions are taken. In China, which is a prime example of one type of communism, the major decisions about major areas of the economy, like electrification, and the size of the armed forces, are taken centrally, while production in most of the country is in the hands of the village communes, or the individual factories. In Yugoslavia the decisions are taken locally, and transmitted to the centre. In the USSR, by contrast, the major decisions are taken at the centre by the Planning Commission, and each unit of production is given detailed instructions as to its output targets. These targets are carefully fitted in to each other, so that the economic system as a whole is completed like a jigsaw puzzle.

At the opposite extreme are economies such as those of Britain or America in the 1860s. There the state did not interfere in the economy, save to raise a (small) revenue for its own (small) expenses—chiefly a standing army. The currency was regulated by the Bank of England in Britain, or by the Treasury in the USA, and everything else was left to individual businessmen who decided how much to produce, and at what price to sell it. In such an economy—a capitalist or market economy—the price is settled by a combination of the cost of production (the supply price) and the amount people are prepared to pay (the effective demand at a given price). Price is not fixed, but is determined by the interaction of supply and demand. A rising price is a sign to producers to produce more, and to consumers to demand less.

Modern 'capitalist' economies are not like this. The principal decisions about major economic matters are taken by the government, which owns and controls a great deal of the economy. Beyond that, the major decisions about industry and agriculture and some of the service sector are taken by large companies, which are characterised by a fragmented ownership (much of it held by financial institutions like insurance companies) and a strong managerial group. These managers deal with consumers, who are often relatively unorganised, and whose tastes are formed partly by persuasive advertising, and with trade unions, which are extremely powerful, especially in setting relative wage and salary levels.

Thus, though there is a distinction between 'command' economies of the Sino-Soviet type, and capitalist or 'market' economies, the distinction does not apply to some crucial economic relationships, especially investment in 'basic' industries. It is a difference that applies, however, to the manner in which decisions are taken, and by whom they are taken, and also to the object of the whole economic exercise. In a command economy the targets are set by the government according to its own judgement of what the objects of society are. For example, in time of war it will be victory and a satisfactory post-war settlement. In Stalin's time in the USSR it was the creation of a massive iron, steel and electricity base. In a market economy, on the other hand, the ultimate aim is to 'satisfy' consumers. It may be that what consumers want is what they have been taught to like by the media, but nevertheless there is a real contrast between a society where few, if any, decisions are left to the individual, and a society where his desires are at least nominally dominant.

Behind all this are traditional societies—economies where the targets have been set by history, where behaviour is determined by duty and obligation, and where output, and the process of production, has a ritual or magic sense. It may be, as many anthropologists have argued, that the modern world will ultimately be seen as a set of examples of these 'primitive' tradition-oriented societies, since much of what we do every day, from the time we get up, to the character of our meals and the clothes that we wear, can be explained as a sort of ritual, to which the simple assumption of economics—that people try to maximise their satisfactions—is not easily and immediately applicable.

## Decision-making

The interesting question, in all these types of economy, is who actually takes economic decisions? This can be posed in two ways. First, who is the actual person who takes the decision (and is the decision a real choice, or is it predetermined?), or, second, are decisions made by one particular class of people? The answer will depend on the type of economic theory to which you subscribe. In the first form of the question, the emphasis is on the quality of the individual's judgement. The great series of technological and industrial revolutions of the past two centuries is seen as a result of individual inventions by people of genius, and the exploitation of these inventions by able and lucky businessmen (or 'entrepreneurs' as they tend to be called in economics—the word means undertakers). The point of a market or free enterprise system is the dispersion of decisions, so that the chances of massive error are cancelled out, as the more accurate judges of the course of events will be rewarded while the less accurate will lose their money. Similarly, in a market economy, each family or individual makes up his own mind what to buy, from his income, faced with the myriad choice of goods and services available at a variety of prices.

In fact, in any actual economy which subscribes to these principles, a number of major decisions are taken by government—for example, negotiations with other countries over foreign trade, and the regulation of some aspects of industry, commerce and agriculture. Most countries of this sort have a social security system which deals with problems of poverty, old age and sickness, and all countries have a state education system. There is also a strong tendency for certain branches of industry to be monopolised, to come under the control of big business, or for the major decisions on pricing and investment to be decided by a cartel, or group of firms acting in concert. Often these cartels are government-supported and even government-organised. Workers, too, are for the most part organised in trade unions and negotiations about conditions of work and wages are conducted with employers on their behalf; they do not negotiate as individuals.

Thus, while in principle there is a dispersion of power under a market economy, in practice much of it is centralised. In a Soviet-type economy, or a 'command economy', a phrase which describes economies of all countries when they are at war, the decisions as to output, investment in new capital goods, employment, prices and wages, are taken by central organs of government to a varying degree. In practice this control is limited by the capacity of bureaucratic organisations to take more than a certain number of decisions, and so those that are taken centrally are those that are considered to be of central importance—the rate of investment in energy, in transport and in steel, for instance—while other decisions, such as the kind of television receivers to be made available, are made at a level nearer the particular factories concerned.

In all communist economies two major sectors—agriculture and retail distribution—have proved intractable, because they involve the employment of a large number of highly individualistic people in conditions which are unstandardised. In the USSR, after nearly 60 years of communism, it has proved virtually impossible to control agricultural production, despite an enormous and sustained campaign of violence against the peasants, and in almost all command economies it has been found inevitable and even desirable that large parts of agriculture are left to individual decisions. The same applies, though to a lesser extent, to individual retailing and small craft businesses.

In part, of course, this represents the persistence of traditions of economic activity which have endured for many generations and which are extremely powerful. Only the market seems to have been successful in altering traditional modes of production and pricing but, as was seen during the industrial and agrarian revolutions in Britain, at considerable cost in social upheaval. All change is disruptive and most change is resented by large groups of people. It follows that any process of economic change, whether beneficent in the long run or not, has an adverse initial impact which causes deep resentments.

## The basic economic problems

Though economies differ profoundly in their technology and in their organisation, there are certain perennial problems that arise, which do not necessarily have to be settled according to some set of general laws, but which nevertheless have to be answered. Who is to do the work, what kinds of work and how much? Who is to own the means of production—the fields and the factories, the ploughs and the trucks? What goods and services are to be produced and in what quantities? Who is to have the right to use or consume these goods and services and on what terms?

Thus in medieval times, it was the serfs and villeins who worked, while the feudal lords owned the land, and small craftsmen and farmers owned the means of production. The serfs were entitled to a marginal subsistence, and when the harvest was poor they died in great numbers, while the whole surplus of society was devoted to the use of the church and the feudal lords. What they wanted—or what custom told them they wanted—was what society produced. In modern market and socialist economics every adult, except a proportion of women, is expected to work. In some sense, what they consume is related to what they are paid, and what they are paid is called their 'earnings', implying a close relationship between work and consumption. Yet these earnings have a large proportion deducted from them in taxation, which is then used for state purposes like defence, education and health, and also to increase (often from zero) the incomes of those who either do not work or who, while working, earn insufficient to keep themselves at the customary and accepted standard of living. So one further series of decisions that economists are interested in is not only who is to do the work, but in what way work is to be related to ultimate consumption. And, in turn, it has to be decided what goods and services are to be made available. In some societies certain kinds of goods are absolutely prohibited —narcotics in the USA, alcohol in Saudi Arabia and contraceptives in the Irish Republic—while elsewhere the decisions are taken centrally. In market economies the individual is encouraged to choose; but the choice is dramatically modified by custom and persuasion.

In a society where all desires were dominated by custom and where the fruits of the earth were liberally available, as they probably were in parts of Polynesia before the European settlement, there would be no economic problems, since there would be no need to choose between pineapples, sucking pig and passion fruit, or between work and play; everything would be available for the gathering or catching. What links all economies where economic problems exist is the problem of choice —between working and not working, between capital and consumption goods, between present and future, and between different types of goods and services. These problems arise because there is scarcity in relation to needs. The scarcity need not be absolute, because a Polynesian with a simple diet and a thatched hut may feel amply satisfied, while a prosperous New York doctor with abundant houseroom, too much food, and a plenitude of electronic equipment may find it hard to support his ex-wives. It is a scarcity relative to social and subjective demands or *needs*. What is a 'demand' in one generation—a TV set for example—becomes a necessity, or an object of 'need' in the next.

The economic problem, then, is to allocate work and the services of capital goods, like machines and trucks, to the production of different sets of goods and services, because if more of commodity *a* is produced, less of commodity *b* is available. We see this most vividly in daily life when the desire to have a better Health Service means higher taxes which leave us less to spend on our own purposes; or, when we are allocating our own funds, the decision to buy a car means a decision not to have a holiday. The economic problem thus resolves itself into two—what is the logic of choice between alternative ends, with limited resources, and how are these resources to be added to?

Behind these two questions is a complex society, and a number of complex people, whose tasks change and may be changed, with regard to the commodities they want and the work they are prepared to do.

FURTHER READING

A good introduction to the development of economic thought is Joan Robinson's *Economic Philosophy* (Pelican, 1964). An interesting view of economic history is contained in J. Hicks' *A Theory of Economic History* (Oxford, 1969), and John Vaizey's *Capitalism* (Weidenfeld and Nicolson, 1971) traces the development of that form of economy.

2

# How the Economy works

## Introduction

If we are going to discuss some of the great economic issues of our time—for example inflation, and the policies of governments—in a reasonably intelligent way we need a simple conceptual framework. What we are now going to do is to analyse what determines the aggregate level of output, income and employment in an economy.

Macro-economics is the study of economic aggregates. Thus, for example, we will be talking of *consumption*, that is, expenditures by consumers, without worrying precisely which goods or services it is that people are consuming. This is not to say that such matters are not important; but simply that to analyse what is going on in the economy as a whole we have to simplify things, and we do this by aggregation.

The conceptual framework which is set out here is basically that of J. M. Keynes and more precisely that contained in his book *The General Theory of Employment, Interest and Money* which was published in 1936. This is a famous book, partly because it was an intellectual *tour de force*, and partly because most governments in most industrial countries have fairly consistently followed 'Keynesian policies' since 1945 or so. These policies are rather different from those that were pursued before the war and we will point out some of these differences subsequently.

## National Income

The most useful summary measure of the total flow of goods and services produced in each year within a country is the *Gross National Product*. Most countries in the world now produce estimates of their Gross National Product but this is a fairly recent kind of calculation. It was not really until Keynes showed how this aggregate might be regulated that governments went about the production of what we call national accounts in a systematic way. In the United Kingdom the framework of national accounts which we use today was first developed during the Second World War. The precise methods of calculation need not concern us here but essentially the task is to add up the value of all the goods and services produced. In doing this there is an obvious danger of double counting. Take, for example, the car industry: car manufacturers put together components, many of which are produced by other firms. If we add together the output of car manufacturers and the output of their suppliers we have double-counted the latter. To overcome this we add the *net output* of each firm, that is their gross output less the value of goods bought from other industries.

There are also difficulties in valuing the output of parts of the public sector. What is the output of a teacher? To value a car we look at its price, but the teacher's output is not sold—unless he gives private lessons—and thus has no price. The convention used is to assume that his output is equal to his salary. This is very arbitrary but there is no obvious alternative. There are many other problems of valuation and thus the published estimates of the Gross National Product must not be assumed to be perfectly accurate. The statisticians reckon that they are accurate to within ±3% although some economists feel that this overstates the degree of accuracy. The Gross National Product of the United Kingdom in 1975 was £94 095 million.

In producing the annual flow of goods and services we use up some of our stocks of buildings, plant and machinery—they depreciate. So to give an idea of what we are producing out of current effort, or what our production is, net of the run-down of equipment, we can deduct depreciation from the Gross National Product and this gives us a figure for the *Net National Product*. In 1975 this was £83 188 million.

The factors that produce the output are known as *factors of production*. A three-fold classification is normally used: labour, land and capital. The first two are obvious but in economics the term 'capital' takes on a different meaning from that in normal usage. By *capital goods* we mean those goods which are used to produce other goods or services. Typical examples are buildings—houses produce a flow of services which we call housing or accommodation, factories are essential in the production of most goods—and machinery. The owners of each factor gain monetary rewards from production. Labour receives wages and salaries, the owners of land receive rent, and the owners of capital goods receive profits. Now if we leave aside taxes for a moment we can see that the net output of each productive unit must of necessity equal the sum of the payments to the factors that have produced it. If we continue our example of a car manufacturer, and if his net output is, say, £10 million, then part will go to the owners of the land on which it stands, part will go to those who work for the manufacturer and part will accrue as profits. If one thinks about it, where else can the receipts from the sale of the output go? Thus we have an important result: the flow of incomes in aggregate must equal the flow of output. To be more precise *National Income* equals Net National Product. (When we consider things like taxes and incomes we run into estimation problems but these the statisticians adjust for.) Conceptually the two are equal and so they are in practice, when adjustments for taxes and other things have been made. In 1975 the National Income of the United Kingdom was £83 188 million, equal to the Net National Product.

## The problem: what determines the level of national output?

The purpose of this section is to make clear precisely what we mean, in this context, when we ask what determines the level of national output. The question is—why is output high in some years and low in others? There are two other obvious questions that might be asked, both very important, but which are not our principal concern here. The first question is why was the National Income (or Net National Product) £1750 million in 1900 and £83 188 million in 1975? The second: why was the National Income (or Net National Product) of the

United Kingdom in 1972 £48 000 million while that of Greece was 355 000 million Drachmas.

Let us address ourselves—briefly here—to the first question, as it will help us fix ideas in respect of our principal question. The first point is that because we value the flow of incomes or outputs in terms of money value our estimates will be affected by the level of prices. The price level in the United Kingdom in 1975 was very roughly 12½ times greater than the price level ruling in 1900. Thus if we are concerned—as we surely are—with the physical goods and services produced, or with the amount of goods and services that we can purchase with our incomes, it follows that we need to get rid of the effect of prices. One way to do this is to value the Net National Product in 1900 in terms of the price level ruling in 1975. Multiplying the Net National Product of 1900 by 12½ we see that in real terms the Net National Product has increased from £21 875 million to £83 188 million; that is, in real terms the Net National Product has increased about four times. This is a very rough estimate, of course, as the figures for 1900 must be treated as very approximate and it is difficult to compare prices and outputs in years so far apart, as many of the items in the 1975 product were not produced in 1900. However, it does give the rough order of magnitude of the increase in real output.

How did this increase in real output come about? We have seen that there are three factors which produce output—labour, land and capital—and thus increases in output occur either because we have more of these factors or because their quality increases or because we combine them and use them in a more efficient manner. All of these things have occurred. Although it is doubtful whether the area of usable land in Britain has increased significantly this century, the labour force is larger now than it was in 1900 (37% greater, to be precise). It is also clear that we have a much larger stock of capital equipment than we did at the beginning of the century although it is difficult to quantify this increase. The quality of the inputs into the productive process has also improved. This again is fairly self-evident. Due to the rapid expansion of education the average level of education and skill possessed by members of the labour force has increased and, due to scientific and technological advance, the machines we use are far more sophisticated than would have been believed possible in 1900. The sheer efficiency of production has also increased. That is a very rough sketch of the reasons for the growth of output since 1900 and we will return briefly to this, and to the question of international differences in National Income, in Chapter 10.

If we take any economy in any one year (or part of the year) we are entitled to assume that the stock of capital equipment and the stock of technological knowledge are more or less constant. Then, given the number of people who wish to work, the economy can be conceived of as having a level of potential output, that is, the output that could be produced if all its resources were more or less fully utilised. It is never possible, as we shall see, for every worker to be employed—for unemployment to be zero—but if the country is producing at its potential output we would expect unemployment to be low and firms to be producing at close to capacity output. When we look at the record we find that in some years this is so but that in others it is manifestly not so. Which brings us to our central question. Why is it that unemployment is high and firms have considerable excess capacity in some years, while in other years the opposite is true? We are asking: what determines the current level of output in an economy?

To answer this in a meaningful way we need some measure of the degree of slack in the economy. It is possible to measure the degree of utilisation of the capital stock but for our purposes the unemployment rate will be sufficient. The unemployment rate measures as a percentage the unemployed as a proportion of all the potential work force (the employed plus the unemployed). In the post-war period the unemployment rate has fluctuated between 1·2% and 5% which is by historical standards a fairly low overall level of unemployment. If we look, by way of contrast, at the inter-war period we find that the unemployment rate *never* fell below 10%, and rose as high as 22% in 1932, the worst year of the depression. It is these variations in unemployment, and more generally in the level of economic activity that we need to explain. The whole story will unfold in this and the two subsequent chapters. Hence, as we have explained, we aim here to set out the basic idea which we will develop in the following chapters.

## Aggregate demand

Modern (that is post-Keynes) macro-economic theory is conceptually quite simple. The argument is as follows. If we were to observe a single firm which was striving to expand output by taking on more labour, by inducing men to work overtime in the evenings and weekends and was generally using its machines and buildings to the fullest possible extent, and we then asked why this was so, the simple answer would be that demand for the goods produced by the firm was high. Conversely if we see a firm laying off men and generally underutilising its plant and machinery the normal reason for this would be that demand for its goods was too low relative to normal levels of production.

Therefore if we have situations where aggregate employment is low and where aggregate output is below its potential level, the explanation must lie in a deficiency of *aggregate demand*, and vice versa. So to answer our question as to what determines the level of national output we have to look at the components of the aggregate demand for the goods and services of the economy. In looking at these components we are looking (normally on an annual basis) at claims upon the goods and services produced, that is, claims upon the Net National Product.

It is usual to distinguish four such components of aggregate demand: we first list them, and then look at influences on the level of each one. First we have claims made by individuals as consumers. In aggregate we refer to this as *consumption*: normally this is by far the largest claim on goods and services. Second there is *investment*, which in economics means purchases of capital goods. A substantial amount of investment is undertaken by the government (e.g. on roads), but for purposes of classification we shall mean by investment that undertaken by the private sector. Our third component of aggregate demand is government expenditure on goods and services, including capital goods. We specifically exclude the expenditure that the government makes on things like family allowances, pensions and unemployment benefits. Collectively such items are called *transfer payments*, as they involve a transfer of income from tax-payers to other beneficiaries and as such will show up in consumption to the extent that they are spent by the recipients. Thus we only include here expenditure by the government on goods and services such as the purchase of educational services (teachers), administrative services (civil servants), weapons and so on. Finally we come to the fourth component, international trade. Clearly purchases of our goods and services by foreigners—*exports*—represent a claim on the current flow of output. But what about *imports*, purchases by residents of goods and services from abroad? These really represent an addition to the annual flow of output produced within a country, or alternatively they represent a *negative* component of aggregate demand. It is in this latter way that we shall treat them. Thus we have an equation that shows

*Aggregate demand = Consumption + Investment + Government Expenditure on goods and services + Exports − Imports.*

In looking at what determines the level of each component of aggregate demand we have to simplify drastically and throughout if we are to get anywhere. For reasons that will become evident, we are essentially concerned with the way in which each item is affected by the current level of National Income.

The major determinant of a family's level of consumption expenditure will be its income, or more precisely, its disposable (or post-tax) income. To be sure there will be many other influences such as the age of the head of the family, the number of children, whether the family is thrifty and so on. However, when we aggregate all families to derive aggregate consumption these influences will cancel out and so we can take it that consumption depends upon the level of income. The precise form of the relationship is called the *propensity to consume*, i.e. the proportion of income which is consumed. The average propensity to consume of a nation is derived by dividing its consumption by the national income. In the United Kingdom it is roughly 0·78 although the proportion of personal disposable income that is consumed is much higher, about 0·87. There is another dimension to the propensity to consume—*the marginal propensity to consume*. This is the proportion of any *increment* to income which is consumed. For our purposes we can assume that the marginal and the average propensities are equal—which is not far from the truth.

Any income which is not consumed is *savings*. In economics 'savings' is most easily defined as 'not consuming' and in this context it is irrelevant what happens to the savings. It makes no difference whether a person puts his savings in a bank, or buys shares, or puts it under the bed.

There are many influences on the amount of investment undertaken by the private sector and economists are far from clear about the relative importance of each. What is agreed is that investment is the most volatile part of aggregate demand largely because it is based upon firms' expectations of the future (when they will have to sell the goods and services produced by the investment). There are three influences upon the level of investment which have been stressed by economists. The first is the rate of growth of income. The argument here is that the faster income, and hence output, is growing, the greater the stock of capital equipment that will be needed, as presumably there is an engineering relationship in any plant between the stock of machines and the flow of output.

The other two influences on investment pay more attention to the finance of investment. When we look at how firms finance their investment we see that the largest source of funds (around 80%) is profits which have been earned by the firm in previous years but not distributed to shareholders. The larger this accumulated fund of undistributed profits, the argument goes, the higher will be the level of investment. There is clearly something in this reasoning, but the problem is that it does not tell us why the firm should want to invest. What is clear, however, is that firms will find it difficult to finance investment in years following a period when profit levels are very low, such as 1972–4 in the United Kingdom.

The Stock Exchange is now an unimportant source of new finance and consequently firms will have to turn, as they have done increasingly in the past, to the banks for borrowed funds.

The final influence on investment is the rate of interest, although there is disagreement as to how sensitive investment is to the interest rate. Why should it be at all sensitive? The reason is that when a firm invests—equips a new factory, or buys a new machine—it makes, often in a rough and ready way, an estimate of the rate of return on its investment. It pays for the capital goods now and in future it will earn profits on the goods produced and by using certain techniques a rate of return can be estimated. The firm will only make the investment if its percentage return exceeds the cost of the funds used. This is easiest to see where the firm has to borrow the funds; there is not much point in borrowing funds at 10% to undertake investment which yields 5%. Where undistributed profits are used, the link is less obvious, but if the funds were not used for investment purposes they could be lent. Hence the opportunity cost of the funds will be related to the rate of interest. (By *opportunity cost* we mean the cost in terms of the forgone return which would result from lending the money, or investing elsewhere.) Thus the higher the rate of interest the fewer the projects whose return will exceed the interest rate and hence the lower the level of investment.

It is of course also true that the riskier an investment is, the higher the rate of return which will be necessary to induce people to make the gamble.

Now investment decisions take time to make and it is not unrealistic to suppose that the bulk of the investment undertaken in any year reflects decisions made in a previous year. In other words in the short term, with which we are concerned, we can assume that investment is independent of the current level of income (but not of course of previous years' income or of accumulated profits or the interest rate).

The third component of aggregate demand is government expenditure on goods and services. We will assume that, as in the case of investment, the level of government expenditure in any one year is independent of the level of output in that year. This does not seem unreasonable as the level of expenditure in any year is largely predetermined by social and other policies. To be sure, the government, as we shall see, may deliberately change its expenditure in order to influence the level of overall demand and this will clearly have to be allowed for later.

Finally we have to consider exports and imports. There seems no reason to think that the demand from overseas countries for our exports should be related to the level of our income. On the other hand we should expect the level of imports to vary with income even in the short run. Thus when economic activity in a country is high and the level of output (and income) is close to its potential level the level of imports of raw materials and intermediate goods will be relatively high. There will always be a tendency for consumers to spend part of their income on foreign manufactured goods and on holidays abroad. Thus imports of both raw materials and manufactures are likely to vary with income. The relationship is known as the *propensity to import*, and, as in the case of the propensity to consume, we can either talk in terms of the average or of the marginal propensity. Again we shall assume for simplicity, and without doing much violence to the facts, that the average and the marginal propensities are the same. In the United Kingdom the propensity to import is around 0·3.

To sum up so far: there are four components of aggregate demand, one of which, international trade, contains two items —imports and exports. We shall take it that the levels of investment, exports and government expenditure on goods and services do not vary with the short-term level of output but that the levels of consumption and imports do so vary.

## The determination of the equilibrium level of National Product

When we say that the level of aggregate output (Net National Product) is in equilibrium we mean that there are no forces operating either to increase or decrease the level of output.

Such a situation would exist when the aggregate demand for goods and services just equalled the amount of goods and services produced. It may well be that in such a situation there was an excess of demand over output for some particular goods and an excess of output over demand for some other goods but in aggregate the level of demand was just equal to output.

In demonstrating this proposition we will assume for the moment that the price level is constant. This is an assumption which is clearly in contradiction to the facts but its use will, paradoxically, aid our understanding of changes in the price level as well as of the determination of output. Our explanation will centre around a simple numerical example. We will take a case where the annual level of investment is £40 million a year, that of government expenditure on goods and services is £20 million a year, and that of exports is £40 million a year. It will be remembered that we are assuming that these amounts are invariant with the level of income. To keep things simple we will imagine that the government does not raise taxes to finance its expenditure but borrows the funds. Let us suppose that 0·8 of the national income is devoted to consumption and that 0·3 of the national income is spent on imports. With this information we can now draw up a table showing at various levels of National Income or Net National Product how many goods, in aggregate, will be demanded. This is done in Table 1.

The table shows at six different levels of Net National Product what the level of aggregate demand will be on the basis of the information. The figures for aggregate demand in Column (7) are derived by adding Columns (2), (3), (4), (5) and subtracting Column (6) as explained on p. 25. In the final column we show the excess of aggregate demand over the Net National Product at each level of the latter.

It will be seen that only when the Net National Product is £200 million is the level of aggregate demand just adequate. At lower levels of output more goods are demanded than are being produced and at levels of output above £200 million the aggregate demand for goods and services falls short of the amount being produced.

*Table 1*

*All figures are per year and are in £ million*

| (1) *Net National Product (equals National Income)* | (2) *Consumption* | (3) *Investment* | (4) *Government Expenditure on goods and services* | (5) *Exports* | (6) *Imports* | (7) *Aggregate demand* | (8) *Excess of aggregate demand over Net National Product* |
|---|---|---|---|---|---|---|---|
| **140** | 112 | 40 | 20 | 40 | 42 | **170** | 30 |
| **160** | 128 | 40 | 20 | 40 | 48 | **180** | 20 |
| **180** | 144 | 40 | 20 | 40 | 54 | **190** | 10 |
| **200** | 160 | 40 | 20 | 40 | 60 | **200** | 0 |
| **220** | 176 | 40 | 20 | 40 | 66 | **210** | −10 |
| **240** | 192 | 40 | 20 | 40 | 72 | **220** | −20 |

Were the level of output to be different from £200 million then the economy would be out of equilibrium and, most important, in the absence of resource constraints there exist mechanisms to move the level of output (and income) towards £200 million a year. To demonstrate these mechanisms, take first a case where the current level of output is below £200 million, say at £160 million. With output and hence aggregate income at £160 million the total demands for goods and services add up to £180 million. As a group, therefore, manufacturers will tend to suffer a loss of stocks as retailers order more goods to meet the excess demand. For a while this running down of stocks will continue but, as it becomes apparent that the excess demand continues, manufacturers will start to increase production by inducing their work force to work more overtime and by taking on more men. Assuming this is possible (and it will not always be possible) the level of output and income will increase and will tend to go on increasing until output and aggregate demand are brought into line.

Conversely if output is, say, £220 million then as a group firms will not be selling all of the goods and services they are currently producing and will be increasing their holdings of stocks. They will adjust output downwards by reducing average hours of work or by reducing the number of men they employ. Incomes thus fall in line with output and will go on falling until output equals aggregate demand—in our example, at £200 million.

## The multiplier

What happens if there is a change in one form of expenditure? To take a specific example: what would happen to income and output if investment increased to £50 million a year? We might suppose that on balance the managers of firms become, for some reason, more optimistic about the future and as a result decide to invest more in plant and equipment. Table 2 differs then from Table 1 in just one respect. The level of investment is £50 million instead of £40 million. This change demonstrates a normal method of economic analysis, which is to

*Table 2*

*All figures are per year and are in £ million*

| (1) *Net National Product (equals National Income)* | (2) *Consumption* | (3) *Investment* | (4) *Government Expenditure on goods and services* | (5) *Exports* | (6) *Imports* | (7) *Aggregate demand* | (8) *Excess of aggregate demand over Net National Product* |
|---|---|---|---|---|---|---|---|
| **140** | 112 | 50 | 20 | 40 | 42 | **180** | 40 |
| **160** | 128 | 50 | 20 | 40 | 48 | **190** | 30 |
| **180** | 144 | 50 | 20 | 40 | 54 | **200** | 20 |
| **200** | 160 | 50 | 20 | 40 | 60 | **210** | 10 |
| **220** | 176 | 50 | 20 | 40 | 66 | **220** | 0 |
| **240** | 192 | 50 | 20 | 40 | 72 | **230** | —10 |

analyse the effect of varying one factor, holding everything else constant.

As the rate of investment has increased by £10 million and the other components of aggregate demand have not been changed it follows that aggregate demand has increased—at every level of National Income—by £10 million. Thus at the old equilibrium level of Net National Product there is now an excess of aggregate demand over Net National Product and hence this is clearly no longer an equilibrium level of output. We can see in Table 2 that aggregate demand is equal to Net National Product at £220 million and this is where, after a period of time, the level of output will settle. The process may take a little while but we are not concerned here with the path to the new level of output. Thus it is quite possible that before the level of output adjusts to £220 million another independent change may occur to cause output to move towards some other level. We wish to avoid giving the impression, even in such a simplified example as this, that everything works neatly.

As a result of the increase in investment of £10 million, the Net National Product rose, not by £10 million but by £20 million. The same would have been true for any increase in aggregate demand that occurred independently of a change in the level of Net National Product. The tendency for Net National Product to increase by a greater amount than the increase in expenditure is known as the *multiplier*. In our example the multiplier is 2.

What causes this multiple expansion of output? In our example the initial change was an expansion of £10 million in the rate of investment. As firms purchase more machines and construct more factories the incomes of those who produce machines and of the construction industry will rise, ultimately by £10 million. Some of the increase in income will be in the form of wages and salaries and some will be in profits. Now we know that as income rises by £10 million, £8 million of this will be spent (as the propensity to consume is 0·8) and £2 million will be saved. We also know that of the increase in consumption, £3 million will directly or indirectly be spent on imports (as the propensity to import is 0·3). Thus £5 million is spent on home-produced goods and services and there will be a subsequent increase in incomes of those who produce these extra goods and services of £5 million. This subsequent increase in income will be allocated in the same way. Thus £2½ million will be saved or spent on imports leaving £2½ million to be spent on home-produced goods and services. There is thus a third round increase of £2½ million pounds in income and half of this will be passed on; and so the process continues. The process is thus:

| | |
|---|---|
| First round increase in income | £10 million |
| Second round increase in income | £5 million |
| Third round increase in income | £2½ million |
| Fourth round increase in income | £1¼ million |
| Fifth round increase in income | £⅝ million |
| Sixth round increase in income | £$\frac{5}{16}$ million |

and the process continues, although the successive injections to output will become very small. Mathematicians call such a process as this a 'geometric progression' and we know that the sum of all the increases in income in this example will be £20 million, or twice the first round increase in income, which it will be remembered was due to the increase in investment.

What determines the size of the multiplier? It clearly depends upon the proportion of any increase in income that is passed on to other producers in the home economy; that is, it depends on how much is spent on home consumption as opposed to the amounts saved or spent in imports. The latter items can be seen as 'leakages' from the income-generating process—the larger the leakages the smaller the multiplier.[1]

In practice the value of the multiplier is rather smaller than in our example as there are more leakages. The most obvious omission from our example is taxes. If we go back to the initial increase in incomes due to the increase in investment, some of

[1] Formally, the value of the multiplier is given by the reciprocal of the proportion withdrawn from the sequence each round. In this example, where one half is withdrawn, the multiplier is $\frac{1}{\frac{1}{2}} = 2$.

this will be siphoned off by the government in the form of direct taxes (that is, taxes on income). Similarly as the first-round income is spent, some will go on goods which are subject to indirect taxes (such as value added tax or tobacco duty) and thus some lesser amount, depending on the rate of indirect taxation, will be passed on.

There are various other things which affect the value of the multiplier. The upshot of it all is that in the UK the value of the multiplier is roughly 1·4—which means that any increase (decrease) in expenditure will cause a 1·4-fold increase (decrease) in income. To be precise, if the government increases current expenditure on roads by £100 million a year, the net effect on National Income will be an increase of £140 million a year. Thus the value of the multiplier is of crucial importance to the government in its macro-economic policies.

## The equilibrium level of National Income—feasible or desirable?

We have said nothing so far about whether the equilibrium level towards which the level of output and income will tend is either feasible given the resources of the economy, or desirable. To investigate this let us return to the notion of potential output which we introduced above. We saw there, and it is fairly obvious, that there is a limit to the number of goods and services which can be produced in any year. The limits are largely imposed by the amount of available labour and capital and the state of technology. As the latter two limits must be fairly rigid within a period of a year, the operative constraint becomes the amount of labour. That is, although firms are unable to alter their capital equipment significantly in the short run they can work it more intensively by employing more labour. We can therefore define the potential level of output with respect to employment, or more conveniently to unemployment.

We can say that the feasible level of output is that which secures *full employment* and we must now define this state. The simplest way to do this is to break down the total number of unemployed into three groups. In doing this it is important to remember that the statistics of unemployment are derived by counting the number of Insurance Cards deposited at Employment Exchanges by the unemployed. If an unemployed person does not deposit his or her card at an exchange and register as being unemployed then he or she will not count as unemployed. Large groups of workers do not register. Numerically the most important of these are married women; usually they do not qualify for benefit and hence they do not register as unemployed and do not appear in the unemployment statistics. It is for this reason, above all, that the published figures of unemployment need careful interpretation.

Unemployment can be classified—at least conceptually—into three groups: frictional, structural and cyclical. As we look at each group in turn it will be seen that some unemployment is a normal, and even a desirable, feature of a modern industrial economy. The largest group of those unemployed for *frictional* reasons will be people who are changing jobs. When people change jobs they often have a period of perhaps one or two weeks when they are unemployed and are searching for other employment. During this time if they register as unemployed to receive benefit then they will be counted as unemployed. As labour turnover is relatively high—in the United Kingdom it is around 40% a year—it follows that there will always be at any one time a considerable number of people who are simply changing jobs. We also include in frictional unemployment people who are unemployed for seasonal reasons and people who, perhaps due to some disability, find it very difficult to obtain a job at any time. Some clue as to the proportion of the unemployed who are unemployed for these reasons can be gained by looking at the length of time for which people are unemployed. Normally between 25% and 30% of the unemployed at any one time will have been unemployed for less than four weeks and it is not unreasonable to suppose that a large proportion of these will be simply moving between jobs.

A second type of unemployment is termed *structural* unemployment. Here we include people who are unemployed because the industries in which they were working have tended to decline or have changed their structure, for example by using more capital-intensive techniques, in such a way as to reduce their employment. Because the industries which in the United Kingdom have tended to decline over the last thirty or forty years were by and large localised industries, such as coal mining, heavy engineering and ship building, this sort of unemployment tends to be heavily regionalised. Since the war certain areas of the United Kingdom such as the North East coast and Central Scotland, have always experienced relatively high rates of unemployment for this reason. However, we have not sufficient space here to discuss the problem of regional unemployment in detail.

Finally we have what is termed *cyclical* unemployment. Cyclical unemployment is said to exist when there is a deficiency of aggregate demand. In this situation, over and above those people moving between jobs, those people unemployed for seasonal reasons, and those people unemployed because there is a deficiency of the demand for the product of the industry in which they work, there may exist unemployment due to the fact that there is a deficiency of aggregate demand; that is, a deficiency of demand for all products.

Full employment is said to exist when there is no cyclical unemployment. It is difficult to be precise about the number of people who will be unemployed if there is full employment for the simple reason that from the published statistics it is not possible to divide the unemployed neatly into the three groups that we have described above. Further, it is probable that the unemployment rate associated with full employment may change in the course of time. For example, if the agencies whose task it is to speed the movement of workers from one job to another improve their efficiency then the number of people unemployed for frictional reasons would decline. Or, to point out an opposite influence, if the benefit a person receives when he is unemployed is increased as a proportion of his normal wage due to legislation, then there are grounds for believing that men will tend to take longer in moving between jobs.

A very rough indication of when full employment exists can be gained by comparing the numbers of unemployed with the

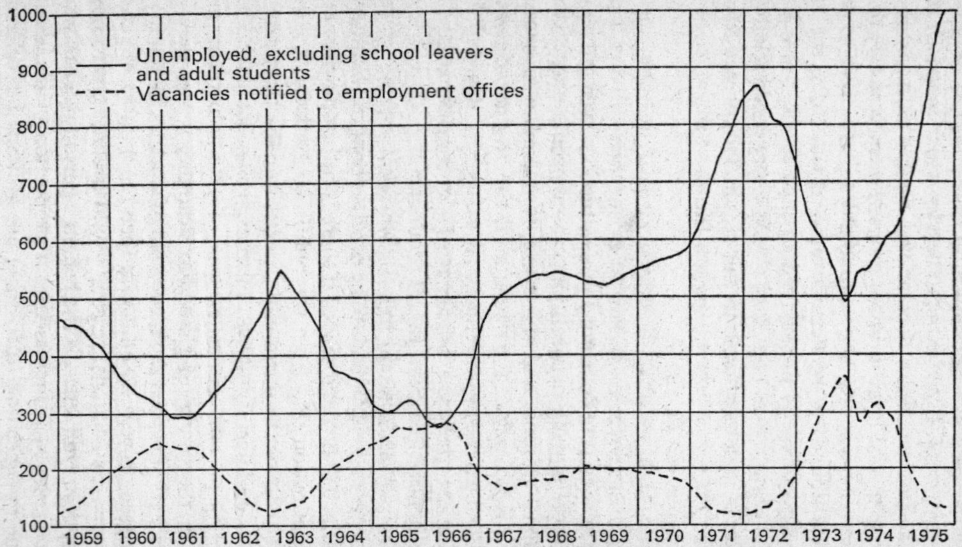


*Figure 1: Unemployed and vacancies in Great Britain 1959–75 (thousands)*
*Source: Department of Employment Gazette*

numbers of vacancies that exist in the economy. This can only be a very rough measure for, as we have explained, the statistics on unemployment have serious limitations and there are similar limitations to the vacancy statistics. The point is that the vacancy statistics are compiled by counting the number of vacancies reported to employment offices and not all vacancies are so notified. In Figure 1 we show the numbers of unemployed and the number of vacancies in the United Kingdom from 1958 to 1975. It can be seen that in 1960 and in 1966 the numbers of unemployed were very roughly equal to the number of vacancies. Thus over the whole economy it could be argued that there was no deficiency of demand for labour and hence there was full employment. In these years there were about 300 000 unemployed, and this was about 1·3% of the total work force. Since 1966 there has not been a year in which there has been a close correspondence between vacancies and unemployment; the nearest was 1973 when there was a difference of just over 100 000. It is now believed that around 1967 there occurred a structural change in the labour market such that after that date the normal level of unemployment was much higher than previously. It is probable that the numbers unemployed when there is full employment in future will tend to be rather higher than the 300 000 or so before 1967.

It is clear from the above discussion that full employment should be interpreted as a band rather than as a point. Bearing this in mind let us return to our problem. We saw in the preceding section that the economy would tend to settle at the level of output (and hence employment) that equated aggregate demand for goods and services with the number of goods and services produced. We have seen in this section that a desirable state of affairs from the point of view of employment would be one in which there was full employment. The problem is that these two levels may not coincide at all, and in fact there is no reason why we should expect them to do so. We thus have three possibilities: one is the happy state where the equilibrium level of output corresponds to that level of output which secures full employment; the second is where the full employment level of output is greater than the equilibrium level of output;

thirdly we have the possibility that the full employment level of output may be below the equilibrium level of output. In the subsequent section we briefly discuss each of the disequilibrium situations.

## Inflation and deflation

Consider again the simple numerical example we had in Table 1.

It will be remembered that this economy will tend to equilibrium at an annual output of £200 million where the aggregate demand for goods and services was equal to the flow of goods and services produced. Now suppose the level of output that would secure full employment was £220 million. In this case there would be less than full employment. Not only would unemployment be relatively high but, remembering that the level of unemployment is but one indicator of potential output, most firms would be working their plants below capacity output. In other words there would be resources unemployed and these would represent an absolute waste. For the country could, given its resources, produce another £20 million of goods and services—it could be that amount better off.

If any economy is in this state we say that it is in *recession*, or, if the under-utilisation of resources is extreme, that it is in a *depression* or a *slump*. The worst slump experienced in industrial countries was in the early 1930s. In the United Kingdom this reached its peak in 1932 when nearly 3 million people, representing 22% of the labour force, were unemployed.

We can anticipate our discussion of government macroeconomic policies in Chapter 4 by briefly looking at the way out of this situation. To get the economy to an output of £220 million we need an addition to aggregate demand of £10 million. For then the economy would be in equilibrium at an output of £220 million. How the government might bring about such an increase in aggregate demand is the subject matter of Chapter 4.

An opposite situation could be where, given the figures in Table 1, the full employment level of output were less than £200 million, say £160 million. Here, as a group, producers would be striving to produce an output of £180 million—for that would be the level of aggregate demand—but the level of output would be limited to around £160 million. It is important to emphasise the word 'around' here, as we have emphasised that full employment (or capacity output) is a range rather than a single point. With an excess of aggregate demand over current levels of output, firms would be working close to full capacity and shortages of goods and services would appear. It is also highly likely that prices would rise. We would have *inflation.* This is the subject matter of the next chapter, but the reader should note that it is possible to have inflation—rising prices—without there being an excess of aggregate demand. In the United Kingdom in 1972 for example retail prices rose by 10·8% when there was an unemployment rate of 3·6%. Excess aggregate demand is but one cause of inflation.

## Summary

We chose to start our book with a discussion of the determinants of the overall level of income and output. The economy is said to be in macro-economic equilibrium when the level of output is just equal to the aggregate demand for goods and services. We have seen that there are two types of instability in the system.

First, there is no reason to expect that at any one time the various actions of consumers, the government, firms, and foreigners should just mesh in to produce a state where aggregate demand equals output. If they do not mesh in, and it is unlikely that they will, then there will be a tendency for output and employment to expand or contract.

Second, the position where the overall demand for goods and services is more or less in line with the production of goods and services may be either not feasible or undesirable. It may not be feasible because there are simply not enough resources to get to that level of output. It may be undesirable because at that level of output there may be unemployed resources.

In the next two chapters we shall build upon this framework to discuss inflation and the methods open to the government in its task of securing macro-economic equilibrium.

### FURTHER READIHG

J. M. Keynes' *The General Theory of Employment, Interest and Money* (Macmillan, 1936) is difficult in places, but is one of the great books. A textbook treatment is provided by W. Beckermen's *An Introduction to National Income Analysis* (second edition, Weidenfeld and Nicolson, 1972).

# 3

# Inflation

## Introduction

Inflation means rising prices. We are devoting a whole chapter to this subject for two reasons. First, as we explain below, during the whole of the post-1945 period it has proved to be the main problem facing the non-Sino-Soviet bloc industrialised countries—those that are conveniently called the OECD countries.[1] Second, since 1970 the world has suffered from an exceptionally high level of inflation, such that for virtually every country the main economic objective is to reduce inflation. Perhaps by the time this book is read this may have been achieved. We sincerely hope it has, but inflation will, we believe, still merit detailed consideration. It has, of course, been notoriously characteristic of Latin America for many decades.

Since the eighteenth century the greater part of the world has been linked by ties of trade and flows of population and capital, or claims to wealth. Since 1917 a growing proportion of the world has insulated itself from this economic system—usually described as 'capitalist'—by adopting various models of communism. But the world outside the Sino-Soviet bloc is probably more tightly linked than ever before. And like any group, it is subject to epidemics. In the 1930s this epidemic was of massive unemployment in the industrialised economies (reaching in 1932–3 one third of all American workers), and of catastrophic price falls for agricultural, mineral and other primary products. This collapse was cured mainly by the Second World War, which was followed by a great world boom

[1] Members of the Organisation for Economic Cooperation and Development. Membership currently comprises Canada, USA, Japan, Australia, New Zealand and virtually all western European countries.

in which rates of economic growth reached unprecedented heights especially in countries like Japan, Spain and Italy which had previously been among the poorest parts of the world industrial economy. This boom in output was accompanied by increases in prices of around 2% to 5% a year. The rate of increase of prices would have been far faster in the 1950s and early 1960s had not a series of agricultural innovations and major mineral discoveries driven the prices of raw materials down. But in the mid-1960s a great boom in raw materials

*Table 3*

*Annual % Change in Retail Prices: Major OECD Countries*

| | *1960–72 average* | *1973* | *1974* | *1975* |
|---|---|---|---|---|
| Canada | 2·3 | 7·6 | 10·8 | 10·8 |
| USA | 2·4 | 6·2 | 11·0 | 9·1 |
| Japan | 5·5 | 11·7 | 24·5 | 11·8 |
| Australia | 3·0 | 9·5 | 15·1 | 15·1 |
| France | 4·3 | 7·3 | 13·7 | 11·7 |
| Germany | 3·0 | 6·9 | 7·0 | 6·0 |
| Italy | 4·1 | 10·8 | 19·1 | 17·0 |
| United Kingdom | 3·8 | 9·2 | 16·0 | 24·2 |
| Belgium | 3·2 | 7·0 | 12·7 | 12·8 |
| Netherlands | 4·7 | 8·0 | 9·6 | 10·2 |
| Sweden | 4·4 | 6·7 | 9·9 | 9·8 |
| All OECD countries | **3·5** | **7·9** | **13·4** | **11·2** |

*Source: OECD Economic Outlook*

prices began, associated with the Vietnam war; American public expenditure grew, as well as that in other countries; and wage settlements which were large by previous standards began to occur on a large scale.

The inflation reached its peak in most, but not all, OECD countries in 1974. Table 3 shows both how the level of inflation in those years was much higher than in the previous decade and how all countries were affected.

We shall examine in this chapter which was the main cause.

Here it is sufficient to say that inflation has now shown itself to be the main problem of the OECD countries. Inflation also worsened in most other countries of the world but throughout this book (with the exception of the last chapter) our main concern is with western industrial economies.

Why is it the central problem? In the nineteenth century the overwhelming problem of the mass of the people was poverty. The great population boom that began in the eighteenth century threatened to overwhelm the means of subsistence; in the 1840s and later, Marx and Engels were still expecting that the mass of the workers would starve. However, the exploitation of America and Australia as sources of food, the development of steam engines and ships, the accumulation of capital and skill avoided this catastrophe, and by the early twentieth century the means of overcoming the problem of poverty were widely available. There followed the depression. That in turn was cured by the discovery, the intellectual basis of which we outlined at the end of the previous chapter, that governments could raise demand to such an extent that all resources could be fully employed. And in the period from 1948 there was a substantial further technological advance, centering on electronics, the car, synthetic fibres and pharmaceuticals, and above all oil and electricity as sources of energy, which transformed the way of life of the whole western world, and of many Third World countries associated with them.

The plan of this chapter is as follows: in the next section we discuss the characteristics of inflation and explain why all but moderate levels of inflation are normally thought to be disadvantageous. We then devote a section to each of the three major explanations of inflation. It will become apparent that they are not necessarily mutually exclusive and that in any one inflation, elements of each may be present. It should also be apparent that we could make the list longer than three. Next, we return to the theme of this introduction—that inflation becomes transmitted to all major industrial countries. In the final section we derive the implications for the control of inflation which arise from each explanation. The details of the associated policy measures will be considered in Chapter 4.

## The characteristics of inflation

We have defined inflation as rising prices; which raises the question of which price-rises we should measure. There are many alternatives, but we will adopt a fairly common convention in measuring the rate of change of the *Retail Price Index* (or its equivalent in other countries).

It is important to understand precisely what this index measures. It measures changes in the prices of goods bought by the typical household. Moreover, the index is weighted according to the expenditure on each item made by the typical household. To show what this means let us imagine we were calculating a price index for just two goods, petrol and tobacco. In the year in which we start our index, that is, the year in which the index will have a value of 100, petrol cost 40p a gallon and tobacco 50p an ounce. In the following year petrol rises by 25% to 50p while tobacco rises by 10% to 55p. The unweighted average price rise of our two commodities is 17½%, therefore an unweighted index would have a value of 117·5. Say the average household spends twice as much a week on petrol as on tobacco. In this case if we are to measure how much more has to be spent to buy the same quantity of goods we ought to 'weight' the petrol price-rise by two, relative to the tobacco price-rise. Thus the weighted increase in prices would be

$$\frac{(25\% \times 2) + (10\% \times 1)}{3} = 20\%$$

and the weighted price index would stand at 120 by the end of the year. Thus the goods which go into the index and the weight assigned to each good reflect average expenditure patterns and need not be completely relevant to any individual. In our example a non-smoking household would be completely unaffected by the rise in the price of tobacco. In recognition of this effect the Department of Employment in England now calculates separate price indices for pensioners, who have expenditure patterns that are significantly different from those of the typical household.

Changes in retail price indices thus give only one measure of inflation and, over long periods of time, as new goods are introduced and as the quality of goods changes, measures of inflation must be interpreted very broadly.

These points should be borne in mind when interpreting the following figures of price inflation in Britain (Table 4).

*Table 4*

*Average Annual Change in Retail Prices, Britain, 1900–75*

| | % | | % |
|---|---|---|---|
| 1900–14 | 0·9 | 1965–69 | 4·6 |
| 1915–39 | 1·1 | 1970 | 8·5 |
| 1940–44 | 5·3 | 1971 | 8·2 |
| 1945–49 | 4·7 | 1972 | 10·8 |
| 1950–54 | 5·6 | 1973 | 9·2 |
| 1955–59 | 2·6 | 1974 | 16·0 |
| 1960–64 | 3·5 | 1975 | 24·2 |

*Source: Dept. of Employment Gazette*

We can see that during this century up to 1939 price inflation averaged around 1% a year (in some years prices fell), and from 1940–69 the average rate of inflation was around 4% a year. The figures for the 1970s show both how the level of inflation is high by historic standards and how inflation has accelerated since 1969.

What is wrong with inflation of the sort of level experienced in Britain in the early 1970s or, *a fortiori*, with higher levels of inflation? Perhaps the basic point is that rapid inflation may erode confidence in money. *Money* is traditionally defined as anything which is generally acceptable as a medium of exchange and which acts as a measure of value and as a store of value. The form which money takes has varied from century to century and from society to society, and the dividing line between money and 'non-money' is very hazy. For working purposes we shall take the money supply to comprise notes and coins held by the public plus the public's deposits with banks. Now, money can only perform its functions if it is reasonably stable in value. The value of money is the amount of goods and services a given quantity of money can command and hence is obviously inversely related to the price level. Inflation therefore causes the value of money to decline and if the rate of decline is rapid enough, money may cease to be generally acceptable and this will cause a modern economy, based as it is on the use of money, slowly to cease to function. In extreme inflations—hyperinflations—the economy simply collapses. The most severe hyperinflations were those experienced in some central European countries after the Second World War. The rate of increase in prices experienced then seems unbelievable. In Hungary, for example, between August 1945 and July 1946 the price level increased

38 100 000 000 000 000 000 000 000 000

times. Money ceased to have any meaning and Hungary became a barter economy (the only alternative to a monetary economy).

Second, the effect of inflation is to enrich and impoverish, apparently arbitrarily, different sections of the population. It is soon realised, however, that the relative economic and political strength of organised groups is the major determinant of these relative changes. This calls the political process in question, and makes any form of government, but especially democratic government, more difficult—the result being calls for tyrannical measures to control the inflation. The process of inflation destroys the fiscal and monetary mechanisms of society and disrupts the international mechanisms, thus causing considerable institutional stress. Above all, the continual shifts in the value of money unsettle long-established habits and values, and may contribute to a breakdown of society.

A rapid rise in prices undermines confidence. A constellation of prices—where things have a known and steady price—seems to be part of the necessary set-up of a stable and acceptable society. Inflation has the effect of reducing the value of all assets fixed in money terms, and this applies especially, of course, to small savers, who invest, for example, in government securities. Inflation also harshly affects all those whose money incomes are fixed in money terms; and it benefits those who are able to gain money income rises above the average.

Inflation proceeds in a leapfrogging process. Prices that can be adjusted daily, as in markets for vegetables, rise daily; prices that can only be changed occasionally (like postage stamps) change by big jumps periodically. This makes all form of planning difficult, whether personal or corporate; and it effectively damages to the point of destruction the allocation function of the price level.

However, inflation is not to be deprecated because it impoverishes the poor or enriches the rich, as groups; it probably does not. It is its chance elevation of some and ruin of others that is at the heart of its destructiveness.

One redistribution which inflation causes, and which is not arbitrary because it is predictable, is from creditors to debtors. It means that debtors can borrow £100 and in effect, some years later, pay back much less, while (conversely) creditors lose the equivalent to the sum the debtors gain. Inflation is thus normally—but not always—good for profit, since profit represents the gap between what has been spent (which is mostly in the past, when the price level was lower) and what is earned now, when prices are higher. In so far, therefore, as the 'animal spirits' of businessmen depend on the outlook for profits, inflation is likely to make businessmen more cheerful.

But businessmen are also people who suffer wet and cold like the rest of us, as Shylock reminds us, and therefore they grow apprehensive because their costs are out of control and they know that if they agree to any fixed-cost contracts in the future they will be unable to fulfil them. Their assets held in money also fall in value as the price level rises.

Inflation's other major disadvantage is its effect on foreign trade. A country experiencing a more rapid rate of inflation than its overseas competitors will find it difficult to export, while imported goods will become more attractive as the prices of domestic goods rise relatively. Through a mechanism which we explain in Chapter 9, the external value of the currency falls at first gradually, then quickly. People seek to retain foreign earnings overseas, and to flee from their own currency; and the same is true of foreigners.

This is not to argue that some mild degree of inflation may not be beneficial: in a world where prices are fairly inflexible downwards a mild inflation makes it easier to bring about relative price changes. Mild inflation may also increase business optimism. Beyond a certain point, however, these advantages are outweighed by the adverse effects which we have discussed.

We should finally mention that it is possible to argue that any level of inflation is tolerable as long as it is perfectly anticipated by everybody. That is, if everyone *knew* that inflation was going to be 100% a year for the next ten years all monetary contracts could be adjusted accordingly. This is sound as a logical proposition but the evidence shows that the rate of inflation is rarely anticipated.

Ultimately, of course, any inflation has to end. All known hyperinflations have been succeeded by a major economic recession, and major political change. If inflation were permanent, social institutions would perhaps adapt to it, as they have in Brazil, where it is assumed that the value of money will change, but usually its transience is perhaps the most unnerving thing of all.

## The 'excess demand' theory of inflation

There are three major explanations of inflation and there is some evidence to support all of them. In general, it is widely agreed that in markets where prices are not fixed by the producer, especially in primary product markets, a rise in demand which is not matched by a rise in supply will lead to a rise in prices. If this applies to a whole series of primary products, as in the later stages of the boom of the 1960s, or in the rearmament boom of 1950–1, then there will be a tendency for all prices in the industrial countries to rise.

It was argued for many years that the cause of the gentle but accelerating price rise of the post-1947 period in most western industrial countries was due to a general condition of excess demand, in which all commodities and goods were subject to a steady condition of being in slightly short supply relative to the rising demand. In terms of the static analysis presented in the previous chapter the level of aggregate demand was slightly in excess of aggregate output at full employment, causing prices to rise.

It was argued that the remedy for inflation, therefore, was to reduce slightly the pressure of demand. The reasons why excess aggregate demand causes prices to rise are simple. At any point in time the possibilities of production from a given set of capital equipment, natural resources and labour are more or less fixed. If an economy starts from a level of serious unemployment of equipment and labour, then additional effective demand will lead to rising output. Employment will rise, and as that happens, profits will also rise. So the resistance to wage demands will fall. Gradually, as demand increases, further increases in output will become more and more difficult—people will work overtime, retired people will return to work, married women with children will take part-time work, so that though the labour force grows it does so with greater difficulty. Bottlenecks appear in supplies; the prices of raw materials sold on the open market rise; interest rates tend to go up—and all this leads to a tendency for prices to rise. After a point, output can only increase slightly as the level of 'full' employment is reached, and the extra demand for goods and services pushes up those prices that are set by market bargaining. This increases the prices of those commodities which enter into the costs of products, chiefly manufactured goods, whose prices are fixed on a cost plus a rate of profit basis. Thus the process of inflation is associated with rising demand; as demand increases, so prices begin to rise with output.

This increase in aggregate demand is usually associated with government, for if it were to be done in the private sector, the failure of investment to yield a corresponding rise in profitable output—as costs rise faster than profits—would lead to failed expectations, and so a collapse of profits. But if government is seeking to increase its expenditure beyond the level of possible output, it can print the money to pay for it. This bids resources to the government's purposes away from the private sector,

This in turn raises prices in the private sector, which then bids resources back from the public sector. Often the absurd position arises where different parts of the public sector bid against each other for scarce labour or resources. This happened most vividly in the First World War, before Lloyd George took over as Prime Minister, when the army and navy competed for scarce steel.

The demand theory of inflation in essence describes what happens when government tries to raise its requirements above the capacity of the economy to produce. It is something which has accompanied the wish of governments to spend far more than has been customary, either in war, or in post-Keynesian peacetime. But it has also accompanied the willingness of the monetary authorities to provide the money. The question at issue is whether monetary policy is itself the prime cause of inflation and we return to this in a subsequent part of this chapter.

## Labour market explanations of inflation

The obvious candidate for the simplest explanation of inflation is that it depends upon wage increases. It has already been explained that, in conditions of full employment, there is a perennial temptation for trade unions to push for wage increases—that is, after all, one of the main reasons that they exist at all—and for employers to concede these wage demands without too much of a fight, because, in buoyant trade conditions, most producers can fairly easily sell all they make. As prices are fixed by taking unit costs as labour costs, plus raw materials, plus an on-cost for overheads and profits, a rise in unit labour costs raises prices. To the extent that *labour productivity*—that is the average output produced by each member of the labour force—is rising, any increase in unit labour costs will cause a less-than-proportionate increase in prices. Thus if, over the whole economy, wages rise by 10% a year, then if output per man is rising by 3% a year, firms will on average maintain their profit margins if prices rise by 7%.

It may not be possible for all firms to maintain their profit margins. It is not possible where there is consumer resistance, as in the case of a product losing popularity (for example high-class tailoring), but then the firm eventually goes out of business. In export markets, too, it is difficult to raise prices unless the rate of inflation abroad is equal to or greater than the domestic price rise, unless there is a steady depreciation of the currency. If that is so, then receipts in domestic currency will rise while prices in foreign currency can remain stable. (This is explained fully in Chapter 9.)

This explanation of inflation is similar to the excess demand theory described above. The difference is that here the effect of the excess demand is felt originally in labour markets, causing wages to rise, and these cost increases are then passed on in prices. In pure excess demand theories, product prices are directly affected by the excess demand. As we have indicated, and will explore further in Chapter 5, this will only be true of goods produced by small units whose prices are determined in market situations. Prices of goods produced by large firms are administered prices and are not solely determined by market conditions.

Here the focus is on wages. The notion that there is an inverse relation between wage increases and unemployment was first formalised by Professor A W Phillips in 1958 and is known as the *Phillips curve* (see Figure 2).

Phillips derived this relationship from Victorian data and found that it provided a good explanation of changes in wage rates up to 1957 (when he concluded his study). The point where the curve cuts the horizontal axis, i.e. the level of unemployment at which there would be no increase in wage rates was around 5%. The Phillips curve continued to give a tolerable explanation of changes in both wage rates and wage earnings in Britain up until 1967 (earnings differ from rates in that the former comprise basic rates plus overtime payments, piecework payments, bonuses, etc). From then on the rate of increase of wages was much in excess of that predicted by the Phillips curve from the level of unemployment. For example, in 1972 when the unemployment rate was high by post-war standards at 3·6%, average hourly earnings increased by 15%.

There are several possible reasons for this but the most convincing explanation is that unions and firms have increasingly taken their price expectations into account when bargaining over wages. We discuss this further in the following section.

Others have argued that trade unions have an independent influence on wages—i.e. independent of the state of the labour market—which stems from their bargaining power.

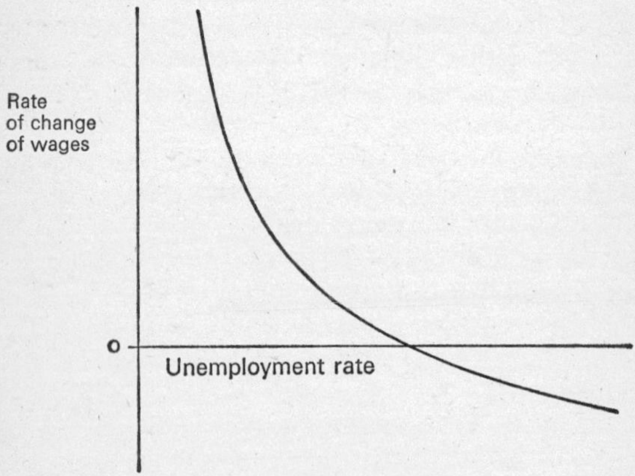


*Figure 2: The Phillips curve*

There is fairly strong evidence that the power of trade unions to demand higher money wages—although not necessarily higher real wages—has grown in countries where labour is allowed to organise freely, regardless of the level of activity in the economy. Thus, while money wage increases are usually highest when the demand for labour is greatest, wages continue to go up even when unemployment is relatively severe. This is in striking contrast to the conditions in the 1920s and early 1930s, even though it was then remarked how little money wages fell considering the depth of the depression. The metaphor was that money wages are 'sticky downwards'. They seem now to have become 'elastic upwards'.

There is strong evidence, which we present in Chapter 8, that wages and salaries are arranged in hicrarchies. While it is true that some groups of workers change their relative position from one decade to another, so that teachers or miners rise or fall in the pecking order, depending upon their relative bargaining strength, the extraordinary fact is the extent to which the greater part of the labour force tends to keep its relative position steady over long periods of time. It is of course difficult to prove this, since the notion of 'employment income' is not a simple one—wage rates, overtime, holiday pay, sickness benefit, working conditions, perks (like lunches and transport) all have to be taken into account. Nevertheless, on the whole the relations including all these qualifications seem to be preserved.

The argument runs that the two principal reasons given by trade unions for a wage increase (and however disguised, almost all claims ultimately are about wages, even if they are ostensibly for shorter hours or longer holidays) are to catch up with price rises, and to keep up with other groups with whom they are comparable. The price rise compensation becomes more and more self-confirming, and of course accelerating if compensation is sought for expected price rises. But the chief factor in wage rises is the argument for comparability. Large groups of workers have their wages settled by arbitration or by quasi-judicial mechanisms. The evidence used for these settlements is almost exclusively comparison with other reference groups. Therefore an attempt to give an extraordinary rise to a low-paid group, or to a group which needs rapidly to attract more workers, is defeated by the fact that other comparable groups immediately press for equivalent rises.

There is in fact an annual wage round, which in many countries is formally recognised, in an attempt to get every group to move together, with a common percentage increase. In the United Kingdom the wage round is spaced out, tending to be led by the stronger and more militant unions, and ending up with the weaker unions, but in this process of follow-my-leader almost inevitably the size of the settlements tends to increase, and the dissatisfaction of those who settled early for less seems to build up, resulting in strikes and a major claim in the next round.

This analysis of how the labour market actually works leads many economists to argue that the process of inflation is associated with the wage structure and that therefore the reform of wage structures and the process of wage bargaining is central to any attempt to control inflation. But according to other economists, this is a description of the mechanism of inflation. Its cause lies elsewhere—in the monetary system.

## The monetary explanation of inflation

To explain fully the monetary view of inflation we must first digress a little and give a brief description of the process by which money is created.

We have already defined money and explained that in a modern economy the forms that money takes are notes and coins in circulation and (by far the larger part) deposits in banks. What we need to know is what causes changes in the supply of money. We begin by looking at how clearing banks—the banks that we see in every High Street—operate.

Banks do not perform a cloakroom function of simply looking after sums deposited with them—they lend the money out in various ways to various institutions and individuals. As we shall see this gives the banking system as a whole the power to 'create' money. In most countries the authorities place restrictions on the way in which banks can hold their assets and this limits their power to create money.

Thus we begin by looking at a balance sheet of a typical bank (Table 5). The terms used are those of the British banking system but the explanation generalises to all systems which have some reserve requirements.

On the left we have the bank's liabilities, which comprise customers' accounts. The right-hand side shows how this money is used. First we have assets defined by the Bank of England (the central bank) as *reserve assets*. The important point here is that each bank must hold at least 12½% of its assets in the form of reserve assets. In our simplified balance sheet there are three reserve assets, which we shall explain in turn. Clearing banks have deposits with the Central Bank, i.e.

the Bank of England, in the same way as we have deposits with clearing banks, and this is the first item. Short-term loans, the second item, are largely loans made to a set of institutions known as the *discount market*. The discount market need not concern us much. Basically the market purchases short-term government securities (particularly those known as Treasury Bills) and it largely finances these purchases by borrowing on a day-to-day basis from the banks. The discount market has, through an agreement with the Bank of England, a virtual

*Table 5*

*Balance Sheet of a Bank*

| **Liabilities** | **Assets** |
|---|---|
| 1 Current accounts | *Reserve assets* |
| 2 Deposit accounts | 1 Balances with the Bank of England |
| | 2 Short-term loans |
| | 3 Short-dated government securities |
| | *Other assets* |
| | 4 Till money |
| | 5 Long-dated government securities |
| | 6 Loans to customers |

monopoly of the original purchase of Treasury Bills and it re-sells some of these to the clearing banks; and their holdings, together with other short-term securities, make up the third item in our balance sheet. This system of having a discount market may strike the reader as odd as it would seem easier for the banks to deal direct with the Bank of England. It is odd: it will suffice to say that most countries get along very nicely without such institutions.

Now we come to the non-reserve assets. Till money is the money banks keep in their branches. Long-dated government securities are those which have more than one year to go before they mature, i.e., are redeemed. *Government securities* are pieces of paper which one receives in return for a loan to the government. One receives a fixed, predetermined rate of interest on them (they are also known as gilt-edged securities: they are gilt-edged in the sense that there is no risk of default but not, as many have found to their cost, in the sense that their market price is in any way guaranteed). They range from short-term stock like Treasury Bills which are three-month loans, through to undated stock like 3½% War Loans which presumably will never be redeemed. Collectively government securities form the largest part of the *National Debt*, the total amount owed by the government to residents and, as some are held by foreigners, to non-residents. (This is not to be confused with inter-government loans which we deal with in Chapter 9.) The National Debt in Britain is around £40 000 million and was largely built up in the Second World War when the money so borrowed financed the war effort. The final item, loans to customers (including firms), requires no explanation.

We are now in a position to see how money can be created. Let us assume that all banks initially are holding just 12½% of their assets as reserve assets, thus meeting the minimum requirements. Now say that into one bank comes a new deposit of £1000 (say from an exporter who has sold goods abroad). This bank's liabilities and assets will both increase by £1000 but it will now have more than 12½% of its assets in the form of reserve assets. As the interest on reserve assets is lower than that on other assets this bank will be in a disequilibrium position. It can meet the reserve assets requirements by keeping £125 (i.e. 12½% of £1000) as reserve assets and increase its loans to customers by £875. The money supply at this point has increased by the initial £1000 (for the original depositor still has £1000) plus the £875 which has been lent to someone else. Assume that this new borrower spends the money on house improvement and that the builder deposits the money with another bank (it does not affect the argument if it is the same bank). This second bank will find its assets and liabilities rising by £875 but need keep only about £109 (12½% of £875) in reserve assets and can lend the remaining £766. It will have created £766 of money. This £766 will eventually find its way into another bank and so the process goes on. The process is thus:

| | |
|---|---|
| Initial increase in money supply | £1,000 |
| Second-round increase in money supply | £875 |
| Third-round increase in money supply | £776 |
| Fourth-round increase in money supply | £679 |

And so on. The reader will note that this is precisely the same sort of sequence as the multiplier process described in Chapter 2, and the sequence sums in the same way. The ultimate increase in the money supply will be eight times the original increase.[1] As in the case of the income multiplier described earlier the value of the money creation multiplier will be lower than in our example as there are leakages out of the process. The more important of these leakages are firstly that most expenditures from loans will have an import content and hence this money will drain out of the domestic system. Secondly our example assumes that recipients of cash deposit all of it in their banks; this will rarely be the case, however, as they will retain some in their pockets or their cash tills. The principle remains, however. For any change (positive or negative) in the reserve assets of the banks the supply of money will change more than proportionately.

We can now return to our main theme. The monetarists believe that trade unions and other institutions are all parts in a play written by the monetary system. It has long been a major strand in economic thinking—almost as old as economics itself—that the volume of money is linked to the level of prices. The gold discoveries in the Americas in the sixteenth century were thought to have caused the sustained price rise throughout Europe in the sixteenth and seventeenth centuries. Money then meant gold coins; the gold looted in America was brought back by the Spanish and Portuguese, and some of it looted in turn by

[1] The value of the multiplier is equal to $\frac{1}{\text{proportion withdrawn}}$; in this case $\frac{1}{12{\cdot}5/100} = 8$.

English and other privateers; this gold was used to buy goods, services and above all property. Prices rose. This theory was called the *Quantity Theory of Money*. It was first really formalised in the early part of this century in the Fisher formula:

$$MV = PT \quad \text{where}$$

- $M$ is the money supply
- $V$ is the velocity of circulation, that is, the number of times each unit of money is used each year
- $P$ is the price level
- $T$ is the number of transactions per year, a concept that was always ambiguous.

The Fisher formula is really an identity, as the left-hand side is the value of monetary transactions in a year, and the right-hand side is the value of goods and services bought. It was turned into a theory, however, by assuming $V$ to be constant and by assuming that (as was the prevailing view before Keynes) the economy would always tend to settle at or around full employment; thus $T$ was, in the short run, always fixed. Thus, given $V$ and $T$, the theory was that changes in $M$ would cause proportionate changes in $P$.

The work of Keynes appeared to destroy this theory as in Keynesian theory $T$ cannot be taken as given and Keynes also believed that $V$ was far from constant. Thus the simple relationship no longer held, although if the economy were at full employment then increases in the money supply would cause (or add to) inflation.

Although what may be termed the 'naïve quantity theory' is discredited, there has been developed a 'new quantity theory' based originally upon the work of Milton Friedman. This has been called the 'monetarist counter-revolution' (against the 'Keynesian revolution'). To attempt to summarise this debate, which is far from settled (although we would guess that the monetarists are winning) would be to go far beyond the scope of this book. We can, however, give a brief sketch of the monetarist position together with a few of the counter-arguments.

The monetarist view asserts that there is a close statistical correlation between movements in the supply of money and the rate of change in National Income (measured in current prices). This is not an immediate connection, as there are lags, which vary from economy to economy and from time to time, but generally speaking, a rise in the money supply seems to be associated with a rise in National Income. We have seen that a rise in National Income measured in current prices could be due to a rise in prices (real output constant) or to a rise in real output (prices constant) or to a combination of both. It is recognised as a weakness of the monetarist position that it gives no clear guide as to which effect is most important, but central to this view is that some of the total effect will be on prices, and thus on the rate of inflation.

The intellectual basis of this association (for statistical correlations prove nothing) is twofold. First that changes in the money supply occur independently of what is going on in the economy—the changes in the money supply following gold discoveries in previous centuries would be an example. Second that the velocity of circulation is constant. The mechanism is then that an addition to the monetary base (reserve assets) will, as we have seen, lead to greater borrowing facilities for consumers and investors. Their expectations of business activity and above all of price rises become more certain; they therefore spend more; and, though some output increases in response to the higher demand, the most immediate effect is a rise in the value of monetary assets, and of property, and then of goods in general.

In an extreme 'Keynesian view' an expansion of the money supply affects the level of economic activity through reducing the rate of interest. We saw in Chapter 2 that a fall in the rate of interest will tend to encourage businessmen to invest; the consequent rise in the incomes of those firms producing capital goods leads to higher consumption; and as real incomes rise, so the trade unions become emboldened to ask for ever higher money wages. As the sensitivity of investment is thought to be small, however, these effects will be fairly weak. The monetarist theory, as we have seen, short-circuits this system by postulating a direct link between a rise in the volume of money and rises in the prices of assets and final goods. These links are established, it is suggested, over a period of years, and are invariable to a fairly close degree.

The great inflations, it is suggested, are a direct result of dramatic increases in the money supply, usually as the result of a war, or some other traumatic event, when government expenditure greatly exceeds tax receipts. The difference, partly made up by printing money, expands the monetary base, and raises prices. Conversely, the great collapse of stockmarket prices in 1929, which triggered off the Great Depression, is held to be due to a serious contraction of the money supply by the United States banking system.

To keep the system smoothly running, it is necessary, according to this view, to expand the money supply more or less in line with the underlying rate of growth in productivity, which in Great Britain is now about 3% per annum. Any rate of growth of the money supply in excess of this leads to inflation. It follows, then, that the way to restrain inflation is by contracting the money supply, especially by removing the deficit in the budget of the public sector. But too severe a contraction, while bringing the price rise to a screeching halt, will do so in a painful manner because, by a violent shift in expectations, it causes severe bankruptcies and serious unemployment. But it is worth pointing out that such a process is inevitable, in any case, once hyperinflation has begun, because all hyperinflations lead to a major economic collapse.

Fairly central to the monetarist theory of inflation is the role of price expectations; that is, people's expectation of the future level of inflation. It is believed that people by and large can see through the veil of money and are essentially concerned with real quantities. Thus if prices are stable and trade unions are aiming at increasing real wages by 3% this year they will ask for 3% increases in money wages. Now, say they expect that in the coming year prices will rise by 5%. To get a 3% increase in real wages they will have to ask for an 8% rise in money wages. If employers hold the same price expectation they will be willing to concede this as they expect to be able to increase their product prices. The process is self-fulfilling and will lead to an acceleration of inflation.

The key question is how people form their expectations of future prices. From recent research there seems little doubt that expectations are based on past experience but that it takes a little time for expectations to adapt to a change in current conditions.

The monetarists therefore explain the apparent shift in the Phillips relation that we showed in Figure 2 by the fact that trade unions and employers are incorporating price expectations into their bargaining. Basically the expectation hypothesis amounts to little more than saying that an inflation once started will accelerate, but it carries an important policy implication in that price expectations have to be 'shaken down'. As to the monetarist the cause of inflation is a too rapid expansion of the money supply, it follows that a reduction in its rate of growth with consequent increases in unemployment is necessary. One does not have to be a supporter of these monetary theories to see the importance of reducing price expectations. Thus those who believe in prices and incomes policies argue that a short, sharp reduction in inflation which the policies bring has this beneficial effect.

We saw that the monetarist view of the economy rested upon two assumptions; first, that the velocity of circulation would be taken as constant. Although not always clear cut, the weight of evidence suggests that this is a reasonable assumption. The second was that the money supply changes independently of the state of the economy. This is crucial. For if the authorities play a purely passive role and increase the money supply when the demand for money rises in line with National Income then the causal relationship is from income to money, the opposite to that postulated by the monetarists. It is clear that in the United Kingdom, at least up to the early 1970s, changes in the money supply did reflect the level of economic activity although these changes may in turn affect economic activity.

We will discuss the relationship of each of these three explanations to each other in the last section. Here we will end by saying that it is common to all three that whatever the cause of inflation, no inflation can continue unless it is accompanied by an increase in the money supply.

## Sectoral influences on inflation

In this section we briefly outline some mechanisms by which inflation is transmitted within an economy and between economies. For example, it may be shown that the major increase in oil prices that took place as the result of the Middle East war of 1973 led to big increases in the cost of energy. This leads, in turn, to substantial increases in costs in parts of the economy which are heavy energy users—transport and steel. These rises in costs are transformed into price rises which in turn are passed on to other sectors of the economy, leading to a rise in prices which is general but skewed in particular directions.

Another instance of this is the periodic upsurge in the prices of raw materials and food. The long-term cost-curve of most agricultural and mineral products has been downwards for the last 150 years, but when industrial activity is high, the demand for raw materials like oil, coal, wool, cocoa, tin, copper and other minerals rises; and since the possibility of rapidly increasing output is low in many cases, and since the prices of these commodities are normally determined by world commodity markets, by auction in many cases, then the prices rise immediately. Producers of manufactured products begin to build up stocks, which pushes prices up even further. It follows, therefore, that a high and rising level of economic activity in the industrial sectors of the economy causes disproportionate rises in the prices of raw materials. This raises the costs of the manufacturing sector of the economy, and they in turn have to increase their prices, since their prices are determined on a cost-plus-a-rate-of-profit basis.

Thus any 'bottleneck' in the economy can cause a series of subsequent price rises through the economy; and this applies especially to labour. If certain key groups in the economy, frequently the engineers, or the miners (when fuel is scarce), hold out for high wage settlements, then the rest of the economy tends to pass these price rises on. This shows an interesting characteristic of modern economies which is that prices are sticky downwards and that once a price rise has occurred in one sector, it tends to edge up prices throughout the system.

The sectoral model of the way in which inflation occurs points to the way in which it is transmitted internationally. The OECD world, and to some extent the world as a whole, is one economic unit. Some countries, like The Republic of Eire and the Netherlands for example, are so tightly netted into the world economy that the greater part of their economic activity is strictly speaking extra-territorial, and the same is only marginally less true of big economies like those of Germany, Canada and the United Kingdom. It follows, then, that economic events in one country, especially if it is a major country, have repercussions on all other countries, directly proportional to the extent to which other countries are involved in world trade. When the United States economy collapsed in 1929–33 it led to the virtual collapse of many other economies, ranging from primary producers (as they were then) like Australia and Argentina, to highly industrialised countries like the United Kingdom and Germany. Similarly, in the mid-1960s the United States undertook a massive expansion of its welfare state, and added to this a major war effort in Vietnam, without at the same time increasing taxes to cover the expenditure (on a vast scale) which the government had undertaken. The United States represents almost half the OECD total output and, though it imports a relatively small part of its total consumption, its imports are a large part of total world trade, as are its exports. When the level of activity rose in the United States as a result of the government's increase in expenditure, the price of commodities on world markets also began to rise.

At the same time, through complex mechanisms, the extra money generated to pay for the United States public deficit was also used to acquire assets abroad. This expanded the credit base in other countries as a flow of dollars—at one time one of the most desired and desirable currencies to hold in the world because it was so widely acceptable—meant that the banks had real currency on their books against which they could make loans to their own nationals and to American (or multi-national) firms. Thus, in turn, the level of activity was stimulated in countries in Europe and Asia, as well as those, like Latin America, directly in the United States orbit. As each country moved into the world-wide boom, so it had to pay more per unit for its imports, raising its own costs of production; each country expanded its monetary base; each country, as its boom increased in intensity, found its wage levels rising. This led to a world rise in prices, or a world inflation.

In a situation like this, the relationship between currencies becomes upset, partly by shifts in their relative purchasing power, but chiefly because some countries run up surpluses on their overseas accounts and other countries correspondingly run up deficits. In depressions and inflations the temptation is to overcome a deficit by a *devaluation*; that is, by reducing the value of your own domestic currency in terms of other currencies so as to stimulate exports. Once this is done, the domestic prices of imported goods and commodities rise, and this leads to further pressures for domestically generated inflation, as wage-earners seek to restore their purchasing power, reduced by the rise in prices of imports, by raising their money incomes. The world therefore enters a period when world prices are rising, unless the creditor countries adopt policies which reduce their own price levels. This is not as impossible as it seems to those who have lived almost exclusively in an era of rising prices, since if the cost of imports falls (which happens when the value of a currency in terms of other currencies rises, as by an upwards revaluation), so the price level falls anyway. But if the surplus countries use their surplus in order to start a domestic spending spree, the result is a series of inflationary circles.

In a world where economies are closely interlocked, it follows that an epidemic of inflation, like an epidemic of depression, is almost bound to be world-wide. But the more robust and well-managed economies will survive, as Sweden did in the 1930s, or Germany in the 1960s and 1970s; it is the weak economies that go to the wall.

## The control of inflation

This has been a long chapter so we begin by summarising the three sets of theories of inflation on which we have concentrated. First there was the 'excess demand' theory of inflation, that if aggregate demand came to exceed the level of current output at full employment then there would be upward pressure on prices. Aggregate demand consists of consumption plus investment plus government expenditure on goods and services plus exports minus imports. As we saw in Chapter 2, consumption *depends* upon the level of income and hence is unlikely to be responsible for any autonomous upward shift in demand. We saw in this chapter that a rise in investment, beyond that associated with full employment, is unlikely to be sustained for very long as the marginal profitability of investment will decline. Thus we are left with government expenditure and exports. Exports again are unlikely to be a sustained cause of inflation as inflation will reduce export competitiveness and so essentially the emphasis must be on government expenditure. That is, governments spend more than they receive in taxes.

The second explanation was that as inflation is a monetary phenomenon it has monetary causes. Increases in the money supply cause inflation and changes in the rate of inflation can be traced to changes in the rate of expansion of the money supply.

Thirdly we had labour market theories which range from, on the one hand, the view that excess demand pressures are first felt in the labour market, which leads to an increase in wage rates, which is then reflected in price increases. On the other hand there is the view that it is Trade Unions or bargaining processes more generally that independently force up wages and hence prices.

Put in this, admittedly crude, way it becomes obvious that there is much similarity between these theories. For if, starting from conditions of near full employment, the government runs a budget deficit, it can finance this by printing money or by borrowing. To the extent that some resort has to be made to the printing presses then the credit base of the banking system is expanded and the money supply expands. The labour market comes in now in one of two ways. If labour markets become tight then wages tend to rise and if they remain slack then, *if* the increase in the money supply causes prices to rise, bargainers will adjust their price expectations and, again, wages will rise, causing subsequent price changes.

Thus although we do not wish to argue that there are no important differences between the theories—one obvious difference is that the theories associated with excess aggregate demand cannot cope with situations where this does not exist—some of the differences tend to be semantic. The policy implications of the main views have corresponding similarities and differences. We will take up the details of government policy in the next chapter and here simply sketch the main points—which should be obvious by now.

If excess aggregate demand is seen to be the cause then it should be reduced. If a too-rapid increase in the money supply is seen to be the cause then the rate of expansion should be reduced. If inflation is seen to emanate from bargaining in labour markets then direct controls on wages, and perhaps prices, are needed.

With rare exceptions, all major inflations have ended in a severe depression which has not necessarily lasted a long time. What the depression does, however, is to alter the expectations of all players in the economic game. The workers are more concerned to save jobs than to get wage increases; the employers find their profits squeezed as they are unable to sell their goods; the government is forced to reduce its real expenditure; and the general view is changed from a belief that prices will accelerate, to a growing assurance that they will remain steady or fall.

There is a difference, however, between the ending of a mild inflation, such as that which was experienced in the late 1940s and the early 1950s, at the time of the Korean war, and the ending of a hyperinflation like that of 1923–4 in Germany, or in Germany before 1947. In the one case, prices gradually stopped rising as fast as they had been. In the second case, hyperinflation, it is as though the economy hiccoughed, and then had a heart attack.

It is hard to see how hyperinflation can end otherwise, because it is a fundamental derangement of the currency and requires the currency to be replaced. But up to that point there exists the series of alternative strategies that we have briefly described. In practice more than one technique is usually adopted and instances of successfully curbing a rapid inflation and evading an economic depression are few.

## FURTHER READING

The best book on this subject is J. Flemming's *Inflation* (Oxford, 1972).

# 4

# Managing the Economy

## Introduction

Government is always difficult because to govern is to choose and people do not have clear heads or simple hearts. In the past, government sought only to get resources for its own ends —the monarch's court, and his armies. But modern government seeks not only to finance itself but to organise the economy as well. Just to run itself entails, indeed, running the economy, since about half all economic activity is in the public sector in modern 'mixed' economies. But, further than that, government has economic objectives which are independent of its own direct needs. These include the stability of the economy, and especially the currency, the achievement of full employment, the growth of output, an equitable (or acceptable) distribution of income after tax and social receipts, and an external balance of payments. These aims for an economy might be held, and are, by governments of very different political complexions and by different regimes. In essence, they represent to economists, and to the great majority of the informed polity, the economically most desirable objectives of any industrial or post-industrial society.

So they would have seemed to the economists who wrote about the economy in the nineteenth century before the great growth of state activity which has marked modern times. But to the vast majority of them there would have been a presumption that the economy operating by itself, with a small government, a balanced budget, minimal expenditure, free trade and next to no legislation affecting economic decision-making, would achieve these objectives. An economy with flexible wage rates would achieve full employment, the gold standard (a system by which the domestic money supply moved in line with reserves of gold and hence with the Balance of Payments) automatically prevented external deficits; the management of the currency by the central bank ensured price stability; if people earned what they 'deserved', then they would accept the final pattern of earnings; and businessmen would create enough wealth to ensure a rising standard of living. It has to be said that by and large, in nineteenth-century conditions, this was not an unacceptable way of describing the best years. But in times of depression, which became endemic in the twentieth century, the analysis failed to describe the facts of the case. Combinations of full employment and inflation, and an adverse balance of payments—or unemployment without inflation—showed that there was no obvious reason why it should automatically come out right.

In Chapter 2 we showed the basic causes of these disequilibrium situations and here we discuss the ability of the government to manage the economy so as to attain at least some of its policy objectives. The discussion is in three sections, each devoted to a major method of economic management. The concluding section discusses how successful Western governments have been in their macro-economic management of the economy.

## Macro-economic objectives

In the 1930s the principal enemy of economic, social and political stability was identified as unemployment. It was argued in the late 1930s, as we have seen, that the government, by spending on desirable projects, could raise the level of demand to soak up the unemployed till the level of full employment was reached. This indeed was the case for almost a third of a century. The industrialised world has never seen so sustained a period of full employment and of rapid economic growth as that after 1947. But several other objectives obtruded themselves. The full employment was accompanied in a number of countries by gentle and, later, rapid inflation. The obvious conclusion to draw was that the economy had been overstimulated. It followed that, when prices were rising rapidly, the remedy seemed to be to deflate the economy by reducing the pressure of demand, either by raising taxes, or by reducing public expenditure, or both. Similarly, when demand has been high, the economy has sucked in imports, so that more is owed overseas than is earned by exports. In such circumstances the remedy is either to remove the root cause—high consumer demand—or to adopt a policy of devaluation, or import controls, or tariffs. Apart from the fact that the last two policies breach many international treaties, and are illegal under EEC law in Europe, the adoption of such policies invites retaliatory action by overseas countries, and thus defeats its own purpose, by diminishing the volume of world trade.

Thus the pursuit of full employment is only partially compatible with the target of stable prices, and with the target of maintaining an external balance. A government has to pick its way carefully along a path which comes close to all these objectives, veering sometimes nearer one and further from the others. And it is fair to say that there are many places on the economic map marked 'unknown', so that mischance plays a major part in determining what actually happens.

The major long-term objective of governments in most industrial countries has been the maintenance of full employment, although on occasions this objective has had to be sacrificed in favour of some other. It has essentially been an objective of post-war policy—in Britain it was first explicitly set out in the 1944 White Paper on Employment, for example. In terms of the analysis set out in Chapter 2 the aim is to make sure that at the full employment level of output, aggregate demand is just sufficient to take up that output.

Economic management is easiest when one instrument is devoted to attaining each objective. For example, if full employment can be attained by nicely balancing the level of taxes and of public expenditure, then it may be necessary to achieve price stability by the use of an incomes and prices policy, and to seek to maintain the external balance of the economy between imports and exports by adopting a suitable exchange rates policy. In fact, however, each major policy instrument has multiple objectives. For instance, government expenditure is not only undertaken in order to boost employment: it has objectives of its own, such as the building of motorways, or the development of new aircraft. These objectives must be met almost regardless of the coincidental fact that the expenditure also serves the ends of macro-economic policy.

Thus, the idea of maintaining a direct link between one policy objective and one policy instrument is usually not practicable. But it is a great help to clear thinking so to allocate the roles in the economic management drama, because it helps in the formulation of policy to think in these terms. Despite the fact that the objectives are complex, and the pressures of expediency modify the extent to which instruments can be used to achieve them, the establishment of a model of the sort described here enables the issues in question to be presented clearly to the public.

## The maintenance of full employment

The government has sought for many years to maintain equilibrium between the demand for goods and services and their supply, at a reasonably stable price level, with the economy in external balance. The achievement of this constellation of policies is not feasible, it is thought, by the operation of a freely moving private enterprise economy, but has to be the result of government policies. The aim of policy, therefore, is to assess the volume of total output at full-employment level, and the likely level of demand as a result of the action of known forces in the economy.

Our explanation in Chapter 2 was centred around a static situation with known relationships between, for example, national income and the volume of imports. In practice, *forecasts* based on past experience are required of the likely levels of private and public investment, of the total level of private consumption, and of public expenditure. These forecasts also entail guesses as to the level of imports and exports. Some of these estimates can be reasonably precise: for example, the investment intentions of the nationalised industries are known, and private consumption changes only very slowly from year to year, because in normal times people's incomes are reasonably stable and their spending habits change surprisingly slowly year by year. But exports and to some extent imports are only predictable within very broad margins of error. Investment in physical capital—factories, plant and machinery, houses and other building—is volatile; it responds to hopes and fears in an exaggerated form. It follows, therefore, that though the forecast of the economy looks reasonably precise, it contains elements which are necessarily imprecise guesses.

These guesses show a positive or negative balance. Either too much or too little is being demanded of the productive capacity of the economy: if it is the first, then there will tend to be inflation and a balance-of-payments deficit, and if it is the second then there will tend to be unemployment and a balance-of-payments surplus. The job of the budget is to weight the balance of the scales in the opposite direction, to ensure neither over-full nor too little employment. In fact, for thirty years, the official guesses have usually been incorrect. The effect of the measures taken in the budgets, which used to be annual, has sometimes been to destabilise the economy, as we explain later in this chapter. It follows from this experience that the task of seeking to balance aggregate demand and supply at the point of full employment is a very tricky one. The ways in which it might be done vary. They fall into three main categories—the use of the budget, the control of money and direct controls. All three measures tend to be used together, but it is convenient to deal with them separately. They share the aim of reducing aggregate demand if it exceeds aggregate output at current prices and of increasing aggregate demand if it is less than aggregate output.

## Budgetary policy

The use of the budget to control the economy has been Keynesian (and Swedish) orthodoxy for about forty years. The principles behind this view have just been expounded. The budget is directly within the government's control. It is an historic constitutional right of the legislature to control expenditure and to levy taxes; it is an accepted mode of political practice for the Chancellor of the Exchequer—a senior member of the government—to make an annual stock-taking speech, to propose policies, and for his department, the Treasury, to impose its financial control on other departments—even on those, like the Home Office and the Foreign Office, which are as politically powerful as the Treasury itself. Thus, the forces of history have pointed inexorably to the British political tradition and to the Budget as the chief instrument of political economic policy. By gradual extension, its role has shifted from the regulation of the government's own finances to the regulation of the economy as a whole.

To reduce aggregate demand, the government aims to increase tax revenue or reduce its own expenditure and vice versa. It used to be the height of prudence to balance the budget but this, *per se*, is no longer necessarily desirable. Budget deficits and surpluses are deliberately aimed at according to the state of the economy.

The government can then affect aggregate demand, subject to the errors of forecasting and to what is politically possible, by altering taxes and expenditure. The machinery for the collection of taxes is complex and some (for example income tax) can practically only be altered annually. Indirect taxes, like the sales taxes on commodities and services (value added tax), and the excise duties on drink or tobacco, may arouse consumer and political resistance. In countering inflation, increases in indirect taxes suffer from the disadvantage that although they reduce aggregate demand they also increase retail prices and, to the extent that trade unions seek to compensate for price changes, they may add to the pressure of wage demands. In the extreme cases where wages are indexed to prices, as in Australia in 1975–6, changes in indirect taxes are directly reflected in prices. Direct taxes on income, which are of various kinds, may discourage effort, and have considerable adverse effects, when people believe they are paying more tax than they really are. Another problem with taxes is that their yield is often uncertain (since the rate of inflation is not known, for instance, the yield of income taxes is unpredictable), and often deferred. Profits are necessarily taxed retrospectively.

The control of expenditure is even more difficult. The only

way to stop government expenditure is to change policy—for example, to raise all council house rents and eliminate subsidies, or by changing student grants into loans—because small cuts in the estimates of future expenditure have been shown to be merely deferrals. And there is some expenditure that cannot be cut without grave risks (on the police, for example), or without changing the law—civil servants have security of tenure. Most expenditure cuts are hypothetical and, if they actually take place, do so a long time after their impact is required.

The budget is a useful and customary tool. Its defects are that it is cumbersome and uncertain. The former defect has been somewhat reduced as budgets have become more frequent, but the uncertainty remains.

## Monetary policy

Monetary policy is the use of variations in the supply of money and in rates of interest to affect the level of economic activity. We need to explain two things. First, how can the government bring about changes in the money supply; and second, how do such changes affect the economy? In Chapter 3 we laid the foundations of an answer to these two questions.

We saw that the ability of the banks to create money depended upon the volume of reserve assets they possess. Hence to vary the money supply the authorities have to alter the volume of reserve assets. Any alteration in the reserve assets of the banks will, we saw, be reflected in a more than proportionate change in the money supply. Here we will show how the authorities can change the banks' reserves, i.e. reserve assets, at the Bank of England. The simplest way, and one which has obvious links with budgetary policy, is for the government to run a budget deficit and to finance this by printing money or, what is virtually the same thing, paying by cheques drawn on the Bank of England. Eventually this money or the cheques will find their way into the banks whose reserve assets will increase, enabling them to extend more credit, creating money.

A second method centres around the use of *Special Deposits*. These are interest-bearing deposits which the banks can be required to make at the Bank of England but which do *not* count as a reserve asset. Thus to contract the money supply the Bank of England requests Special Deposits and, to the extent that the banks previously held reserve assets close to the minimum reserve asset ratio, their reserve assets fall correspondingly and loans must be recalled to restore the ratio. To expand the money supply the authorities can release Special Deposits. There are various other methods the authorities can use, but the essential principle is the same—to expand the volume of reserve assets held by the banks if a monetary expansion is required, and vice versa to contract the money supply.

Normally an expansion of the money supply will be accompanied by a decrease in interest rates and a contraction (or, perhaps, a decrease in the rate of income) in the money supply by a raising of interest rates. The authorities give a lead in this by varying the Bank of England's *Minimum Lending Rate* but the forces of supply and demand (discussed in the next chapter) would normally bring about the required result. These changes in bank interest rates tend to be reflected in other interest rates although the rates of interest offered, and charged, by building societies are relatively 'sticky', in that they change infrequently.

It should not be inferred from the above description that the authorities can precisely bring about their desired changes in the money supply. Banks and other financial institutions may be able to frustrate their intentions, although on the other hand the authorities may back up their actions by 'directives' to the institutions. The authorities, too, have multiple and conflicting objectives which may militate against tight control over the money supply. It is certainly possible to cite times in the last decade when the authorities' control on the money supply seemed to be, at most, tenuous.

The effect of changes in the money supply on the overall level of economic activity is, as we saw in the previous chapter, subject to some dispute. There we saw that it is commonly held that no inflation can proceed for very long unless it is accompanied by monetary expansion, but that the mechanisms by which money changes affect output, employment and prices are not always clear. The argument is probably strongest about how an increase in the supply of money, and decreases in the rates of interest, can cure an economic depression when the level of aggregate demand is deficient. The monetarists believe that the same causal processes work in reverse but 'Keynesians' dispute this. The main cause of a depression, they argue, is pessimistic expectations on the part of firms, and hence a low level of investment, and that making funds available to firms is useless if they have no wish to invest. Thus in this situation, increases in government expenditure are needed. Here we are talking of a depression that is not accompanied by inflation—a situation such as obtained in the 1930s. Where inflation accompanies low levels of output and employment relative to the potential level of those variables the situation is, as we saw in the last chapter, more complex.

The attempt to regulate the economy by the monetary process is thus not simple. Ideally, according to the protagonists of the monetarist theories the budget should be balanced and the supply of money should grow *pari passu* with the growth of the output potential in the economy. If it grows more slowly there will be unemployment, if it grows more quickly there will be inflation. Some would argue that the money supply should grow a little faster than output potential, by 3% say, thus generating 3% inflation. This would be anticipated, so there would be no losers, and the mild inflation would enable relative price changes to be made more easily.

## Direct controls

The third way of running the economy could not be more different from the monetarist view. It is the view that the economy is like an inquisitive child, darting all over the place, and never coming to rest exactly where you want it to unless you tell it what to do. Thus, if the external balance is in deficit, the easiest course to follow is to control imports, either by quotas or by tariffs. If prices are rising, then they can be fixed. If the cause of the price rise is excessive wage increases, then wages can be controlled. If investment is too low, or going into the wrong parts of the economy, it can be controlled.

There are immense advantages in the use of direct controls. They are immediate in their effect, and they can be directed precisely and neatly to their targets. For this reason some direct controls are always used and in emergencies all governments use a whole range of direct controls.

But the arguments against reliance on controls are powerful. First, it is often not the case that the government's diagnosis is exact. The price rise, for example, may be a mere symptom, and tackling it directly may not remove the real cause of the problem. Next, the controls are often easily evaded, requiring more controls, thus expanding the bureaucracy, and bringing the law more and more into contempt, especially when it is openly flouted. This happened with the black market in Europe in the Second World War, and it is very likely to happen with attempts to impose incomes or wages policies. Thirdly, the attempt to regulate the economy by controls feeds on itself, requiring the government ultimately to have not only an economic strategy, but a policy about individual sectors and sub-sectors of the economy. This requires a degree of sophistication most governments rarely have, and which is ideologically unacceptable to large bodies of opinion.

## Stabilisation and destabilisation

Economic policy is not simple, either in conception or in execution. The three major methods of attempting to regulate the economy all have their individual advantages and disadvantages. In combination the advantages and disadvantages can be lessened or compounded. But they all suffer from a general difficulty—the lags in the process. We can distinguish three lags. First there is a time lag between a change in the economy—let us say it is a downturn in aggregate demand—and the recognition of it by policy-makers. This lag is due, of course, to the time it takes to collect and publish statistics. There is a second time lag between recognition of the problem and the introduction of policy measures to cope with it. Lastly, virtually all the measures that we have discussed affect the economy only after long and variable time lags. It is thought, for example, that a change in income tax rates now will affect aggregate demand six to nine months hence. There are also lags in the effect of monetary policy, as we have explained, and even less is known about these.

It is thus apparent that there is a danger that the government may, in trying to even out fluctuations in aggregate demand, actually destabilise the economy. If, for example, unemployment is thought to be too high at present and the government adds to aggregate demand, by the time this has any effect unemployment may be falling sharply (perhaps due to previous policy). The sensitivity of governments to unemployment for political reasons adds to the possibility of such episodes.

There is now, in fact, a substantial body of evidence to suggest that virtually all economic fluctuations in post-war Britain have been due to government management of aggregate demand. This is partly due to a failure to recognise the time lags discussed above and partly because the emphasis given to various and conflicting objectives tends to change.

Certainly it seems that 'fine tuning' of the economy is now beyond our capabilities and this, together with the above conclusion, lends weight to the monetarists' prescription—that the budget ought to be set roughly in balance and the money supply increased by a steady known amount each year.

Nevertheless it would be wrong to be too pessimistic. Full employment, economic growth, the development of international trade and price stability were more or less achieved in OECD countries up to 1970. Only since 1970 has the price level been out of control, and most countries regained their control by the mid-1970s. Seen in the context of the inter-war years, government demand management policy has been wildly successful. Perhaps we have now come to expect too much of it.

FURTHER READING

A. Prest and D. Coppock's *A Manual of Applied Economics* (Weidenfeld and Nicolson).

# 5

# How the Market works

## Introduction

The most fundamental concepts in economics are supply and demand and these are probably the two economic terms that are most familiar to non-economists.

The analysis presented here dates back at least to the turn of the century and, in essence, to the classical economists of the early nineteenth century. They believed, as do many economists today, that supply and demand analysis could be used to answer virtually all micro-economic questions, such as what determines the price of goods, or labour, or shares, or currencies, and what determines the level of output of each good or service. Thus in answering these questions the analysis could be used to explain the allocation of resources within the economy—that is, why more men and machines are devoted to producing cars than sewing machines and so on. In the final section we outline how the price mechanism may operate to allocate resources.

As we shall explain, the theory of supply and demand is only as powerful as this under certain conditions, which are far from being met in a modern industrial economy. One of the most important of these conditions is that markets are composed of very small units of production and consumption so that no one unit can affect the operation of the market. In some markets this is patently not the case. In many markets, e.g. the markets for teachers and doctors, there is virtually only one buyer, the government, and the markets for many consumer goods and capital goods are dominated by a few producers. The special problems posed by the government and by the existence of large firms are discussed in subsequent chapters. We should note here, however, that 32% of the output of manufacturing industry in Britain is produced by the fifty largest firms.

There are many markets, however, where the assumptions

made by supply and demand theory seem to be reasonable approximations to the facts. Examples would be the market for most raw materials, the market for owner-occupied houses, the market for secretarial staff in large cities, and there are countless others.

Neither would we wish to argue that the analysis has no relevance whatsoever in those markets where its conditions are not met. As we shall see, governments have a very sorry record of intervening in markets in apparent ignorance of the laws of supply and demand.

Which brings us to the last thing that we have to say before introducing the reader to what this analysis in fact is. This is that although we shall attempt to present it in a very precise way—there seems little point in doing otherwise—the analysis has to be interpreted in a broad way, as outlining *tendencies* (e.g. a price moving up or down) rather than indicating very precise results.

## Consumer demand

The consumer is faced with a bewildering variety of goods and services which he may buy. For example, even if he decides to allocate a certain proportion of his weekly expenditure to beer he will still, in most cases, have the products of several breweries to choose from and each brewery will offer him a large range of beers. On the other hand he will only have a certain finite sum of money available for consumption. For our purposes we will assume that he has already decided how much to save.

Thus our consumer has a given sum of money to spend in each period, an immense number of goods and services to choose from and the certainty that, given his desire to save and acquire assets, he would like to spend far more than he can. Apart from the super-rich and the monastic there can be very few of us who would not like to be able to buy more (or more expensive) things than we can afford.

We thus have a constrained choice. How do we make the choice? To fix ideas let us take for the moment the case where we are only concerned with choices between types of good (tea, fish, washing powder, haircuts) without worrying about brands. We assume that the consumer tries to maximise the enjoyment (or utility) that he can derive from his fixed expenditure. He will have preferences between different goods and these preferences will no doubt change as the amounts of each good he consumes change. On the other hand the prices of the goods and services will be fixed and will be invariant with the amount he consumes. At this point it is probably easiest to state the result first and then give an intuitive explanation. A consumer will maximise his enjoyment from the expenditure of a fixed amount if between every pair of goods he consumes the rate at which he is willing to substitute one good for another is equal to the ratio of their prices.

Let us see what would be wrong if this were not the case. Say the pair of goods we consider are beer and chocolate. At his present level of weekly consumption, say he values one pint of beer as being worth *to him* ¼ lb chocolate, i.e. if we took a pint of beer away from him per week and gave him ¼ lb chocolate then his enjoyment from consumption of beer and chocolate combined would be unaltered. Now say the price of beer (one pint) is twice that of a ¼ lb chocolate. Then clearly he would be better off consuming less beer and more chocolate: for by consuming one pint of beer less he could buy up to ½ lb chocolate whereas he only requires ¼ lb chocolate to compensate him. As he alters his pattern of consumption by buying less beer and more chocolate it is reasonable to suppose that he will need increasing amounts of chocolate to compensate him for the loss of a pint of beer (the more we have of something the less we value an extra unit and vice versa). But he would continue to gain until the point where he required ½ lb chocolate to compensate for the loss of a pint of beer. At that point his personal evaluation, at the margin, of the two goods would be equal to the market evaluation, i.e. their relative prices. The rule applies for every pair of goods consumed.

To extend this analysis to expensive goods which are bought infrequently, like cars and washing machines, we need to talk in terms of the value and cost of the weekly flow of services that the good provides.

This is what, in a rough and ready way, we subconsciously do. Nobody could act totally in this way as the information is simply not available, and if it were, neither the human brain nor, for that matter, a computer, could cope with it. To see this let us now allow for the existence of different brands of goods. Imagine a consumer considering whether to buy a stereo system consisting of an amplifier, a record deck, a set of speakers and a cartridge. Stockists of such equipment advertise in music magazines and typically might offer 20 kinds of amplifier, 15 decks, 10 speakers and 10 cartridges. The number of possible combinations is thus 30 000. To make a 'rational' choice, information is required not only on the price but also the technical performance of each combination, which is impossible. Virtually all decisions thus have to be made in relative ignorance.

If our consumer manages to allocate his income in an attempt to avoid bad choices and gets to a position where, given the information available to him, he seems to be spending his income in a sensible way, what things might induce him to change his expenditure patterns? Basically, there are three possible influences. First his income might change; second, the prices of goods may alter relative to one another; and third, his preferences may shift. We consider each in turn.

First, his income might change. As long as prices did not change, this would enable him to buy more of all the goods he consumed or to buy some goods and services that he was not at present consuming, or some combination of both. It is not likely that he will change his consumption proportionately. It is possible that there are some goods of which people may consume less as their income increases. Examples are remould tyres and poor cuts of meat. There is also a large range of goods for which consumption would respond very little to a change in income. Basic foodstuffs such as bread, potatoes, tea, coffee are examples. It is unlikely that in response to an increase in real income of 5% many people (or households) would increase their consumption of those items by as much as 5%. Then there are luxury goods which are highly responsive to changes in income, often not being bought at all at low income levels.

Examples are consumer durable goods, entertainment, eating out and foreign travel. The responsiveness of consumer demand for a good to a change in income is known as the *income elasticity of demand.* It is more sensible to talk in terms of consumers as a group than of an individual consumer. If in response to a given proportionate increase (decrease) in income, consumers increase (decrease) the amount they buy more than proportionately, demand is said to be income elastic. If they increase consumption less than proportionately, demand is said to be income inelastic. Those goods for which the demand *falls* as income increases are known as inferior goods.

Second the prices of some of the goods that the consumer purchases may change. In time of increases in the general price level, when we speak of a price of a good rising we mean that its price *relative* to the average price of all other goods has changed. Again the response of a consumer to a price change will vary from good to good and will largely be determined by how many substitutes there are for the good. Let us first make sure that we understand why his demand patterns change at all in response to price changes. If we imagine our consumer to be in the position where for the last units of every pair of goods he consumes, his own subjective valuation of their relative merit is equal to their price ratio, then if the price of a good falls this equilibrium will be disturbed. In the case of the good whose price has fallen, the market will offer him a better rate of exchange than he needs and he will tend to increase the amount of that good that he purchases. The opposite would happen if the price rose.

This will hold for all consumers and thus we have a fundamental result that if the price of a good falls then the amount that consumers buy will tend to rise and vice versa. (It is important to note here that this is essentially an empirical result for it is not possible to prove it by using economic theory.) We will return in the next section to the question of by how much demand will react to price changes.

Finally the consumer's preferences may change and this will alter his expenditure patterns and thus the amount of any good that he buys. The advertising industry exists in order to change consumer preferences and, to the extent that tastes are social, even in the absence of advertising we would expect consumer preferences to shift over time.

## Market demand

In the previous section we looked at the main influences on the demand of a single consumer for individual goods and services. Here we are concerned with all consumers. The concept we wish to introduce here is that of the *demand* for a good or service. The demand for a good is defined as the amount that consumers are able and willing to buy at any given price, other things being equal.

There are several important features of this definition. First, note the words 'able to buy': we are thus talking of effective demand, demand that is backed up by cash. Second, we are mainly concerned with the relationship between demand and price, which leads us on to the phrase 'other things being equal'. We have seen already that income and preferences will also influence demand, so what we do is to assume that these do not change, so that we can concentrate on the link between demand and price. If we are considering the demand for just one good, then another important set of things that we have to hold constant is the price of all other goods. For if the price of a substitute changes then we would expect demand to change: the demand for coal, for example, will be affected by a change in the price of other forms of energy.

We can show the relationship between demand and price in the form of a demand curve such as that in Figure 3. There is no reason to suppose that demand curves are linear—we draw them that way for simplicity.

As price falls then demand will rise. Hence if we hold other things constant, demand will move along the curve in response to a change in the price of this good. (We emphasise again that in a situation where the general price level changes we are talking in terms of changes in relative prices.) If the other things that affect demand change, then the demand curve will shift, as in Figure 4.

The original demand curve, *d*, will shift to $d_1$ if consumers' real income increased, or if the price of a close substitute rose, or if for some reason consumer preferences for this good became stronger. The curve $d_1$ shows that at any price consumers would now buy more of the good. A downward shift of

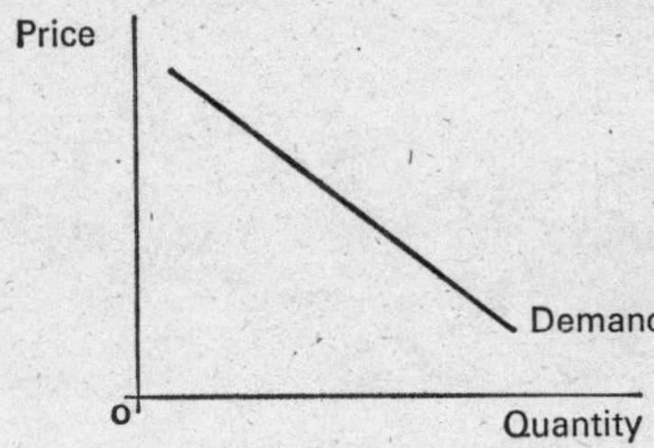


*Figure 3*

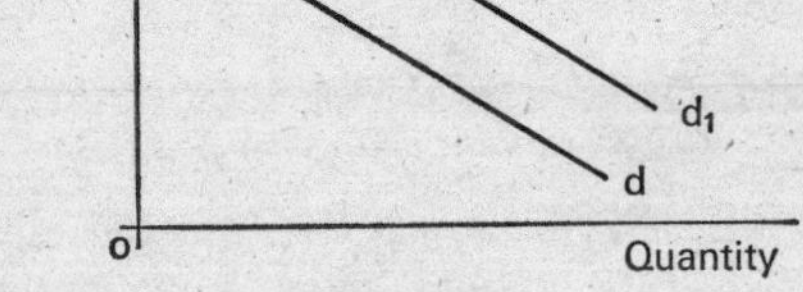


*Figure 4*

the curve to the left of *d*, would have opposite causes and meaning.

The demand for some goods will be sensitive to price, for others it will be fairly insensitive. Compare the two demand curves for goods *x* and *y* in Figure 5.

If the price of each good were originally $p_1$ and the price of each now falls to $p_2$ we see that whereas the demand for *x* increases considerably to $q_3$ that for good *y* only increases slightly to $q_2$. The sensitivity of demand to changes in price is known as the *price elasticity of demand* (the reader will recall that we have already introduced the income elasticity of demand which describes the reaction of demand to changes in income). We say that the demand for a good is price elastic if in

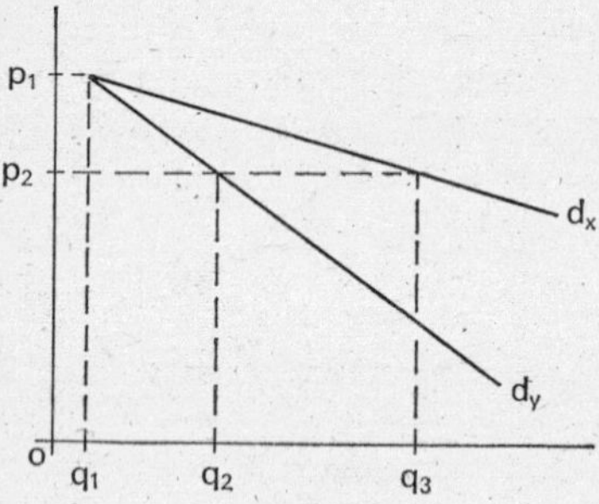


*Figure 5*

response to a decrease in price the amount purchased increases *more than proportionately.* If demand increases less than proportionately then demand is said to be price inelastic. The price elasticity is measured by:

$$\frac{\textit{Proportionate change in quantity demanded}}{\textit{Proportionate change in price}}$$

The result will always be negative and the minus sign is usually neglected. If the result is more than one, then demand is price elastic and if it is less than one then demand is price inelastic.

The main determinant of the price elasticity of demand for a good is the availability of substitutes. If a good has a large number of close substitutes then if its price rises it will be relatively easy for consumers to switch to consuming the alternatives, and vice versa. It follows that in principle most branded goods (e.g. types of washing powder) should have high price elasticities. Firms spend large sums of money, however, on packaging and advertising to persuade people that their brand is different from others. To the extent that they are successful then the price elasticity of demand for each brand will be reduced.

It follows that when we talk of price elasticity we should be careful to specify whether we are talking of a homogeneous good or of a branded good. Thus, the demand for petrol is price inelastic, although the demand for a given brand of petrol is price elastic. Remembering this we can give the following examples of goods for which market demand is price inelastic—basic foodstuffs such as milk, potatoes, bread, sugar, tobacco, alcoholic drinks and petrol.

## Supply

Having seen how buyers behave we now move on to consider the actions of sellers. *Supply* is defined as the amount that sellers are able and willing to sell at any given price. What we wish to do is to derive a supply curve, analogous to the demand curve, so that we can put together the conditions of supply and demand and analyse market behaviour, particularly price determination.

It is in this context that the warnings we gave in the introduction to this chapter become especially important. The analysis presented here only really applies fully in markets in which producers are typically small and act independently of one another. This will be true, as we have explained, in many markets and we will take the case of the production of a basic commodity, say beef.

Suppose the price of beef were to rise significantly. What can we say about the reaction of beef suppliers to this price change? The reaction will vary with time. At any moment there is a stock of beef cattle (for simplicity we consider one country in isolation). Farmers will plan to bring these to the market for sale in an orderly way at the time when they are in prime condition. If the price rises, the weekly supply may increase slightly as animals are sold earlier than had been intended. It is likely, however, that the proportionate response of supply will be less than the proportionate change in price. In the short run, supply is price inelastic. If farmers expect the price change to last into the future, however, they will be able to adjust supply to an increasing extent as time goes on. For beef farming will increase in profitability relative to other forms of livestock production and to arable farming. They will purchase more calves and over a period of years supply will increase in response to the initial price change. We can generalise and say that for most raw materials supply will be price inelastic in the short run but will increase as time proceeds.

Some manufactured goods, such as engineering components, are made by small firms. Here supply is likely to be relatively more responsive to price changes in the short run but, as in the

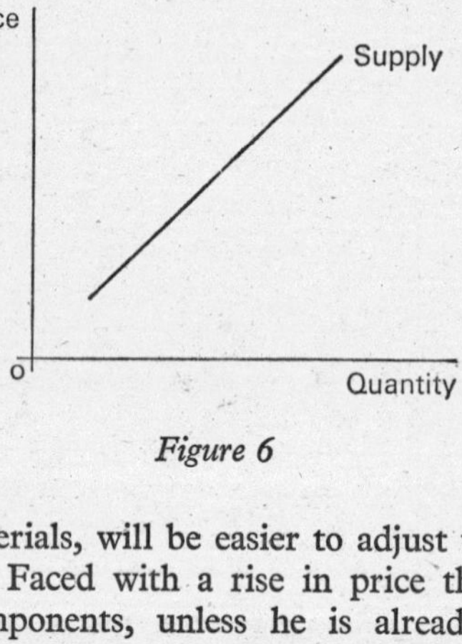


*Figure 6*

case of raw materials, will be easier to adjust the longer the period of time. Faced with a rise in price the supplier of engineering components, unless he is already working at absolute capacity, will be able to increase output by increasing his labour input, either by hiring more men or by inducing his existing labour force to work longer hours. There will be a limit to this increase, however, and this will be given by the physical capacity of his plant. To increase output beyond this will require time to install new equipment and perhaps to extend buildings. Thus, again, the price elasticity of supply will be greater, the longer the period of time over which we measure the supply response.

The above analysis was in terms of a reaction to a price increase but it can be recast in terms of a price decrease. We get the same result. Supply will tend to be higher the greater the price level. We can thus draw a supply curve as in Figure 6. The long run supply curve will always tend to be more responsive to price changes than is the short run curve.

## Supply and demand

We can now bring together the concepts of supply and demand to demonstrate how markets may operate to determine prices and the amounts bought and sold.

Say the market supply and demand for widgets is as given by the two curves in Figure 7.

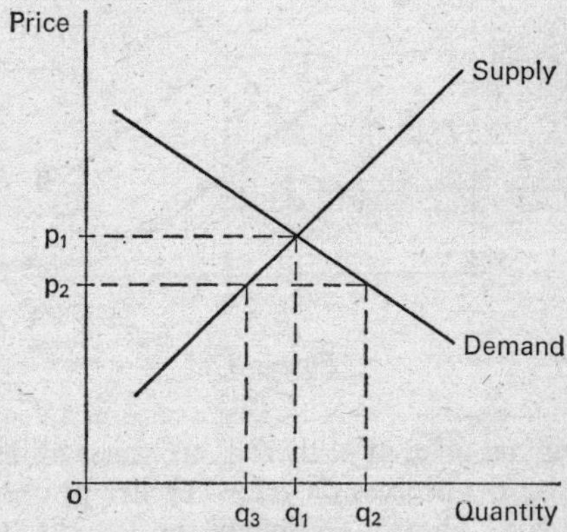


*Figure 7*

The price of widgets will always tend to move towards $p_1$, for only at that price will the amount that suppliers are willing to sell, $q_1$, just equal the amount, $q_1$, that buyers are willing to buy. At that price the market would just be cleared and, in the absence of a shift in market demand or supply, there would be no tendency for price to change.

If the price of widgets were less than $p_1$, say $p_2$, then the market would be in disequilibrium. At that price sellers will be supplying less ($q_3$) than consumers wish to purchase ($q_2$) and there will be an excess demand for widgets. Buyers will tend to offer more and as prices rise then demand falls off. Supply increases, until the price $p_1$ is reached. Were the price to be above $p_1$ to start with, then this process would operate in reverse.

If either the demand or the supply curve shifts then $p_1$ will cease to be an equilibrium price. Take the example shown in Figure 8. Here demand has increased. Consumers are now willing to buy more widgets at any price.

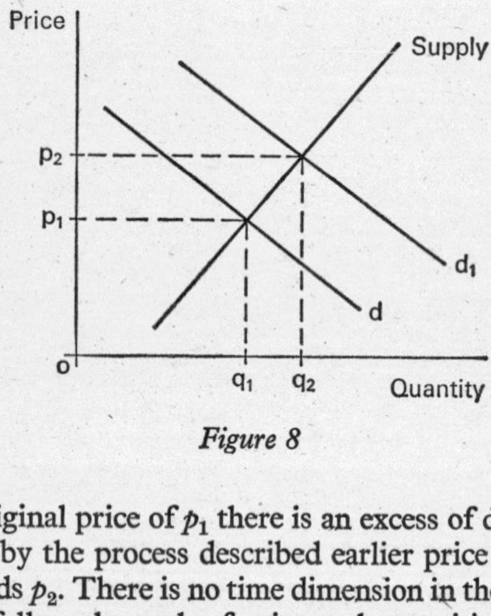


*Figure 8*

At the original price of $p_1$ there is an excess of demand over supply and by the process described earlier price will tend to move towards $p_2$. There is no time dimension in the diagram so we cannot follow the path of price and quantities over time. All we can say is that when a new equilibrium is established it will be at $p_2$. Of course some other change may occur before it is reached. Given the increase in demand the extent of the price change depends upon the elasticity of the supply curve. If sellers find it easy to increase supply in the short run then the price change will be relatively small. If on the other hand sellers can only make marginal adjustments to supply then the price change will be relatively large.

Similarly if we take the case where an equilibrium price is disturbed by a change in supply, then for any given supply change the extent of the price change will be greater the more inelastic is demand.

It is in this way that prices are determined in those markets which approximately meet the assumptions made by the analysis. The important thing to remember is that it is the market, rather than individuals, that sets the price. The price of natural rubber is determined by world supply and demand and the individual plantation in Malaya just has to sell at that price. If it were to set its price higher then no one would buy its rubber. There is also no reason for it to charge a lower price, for it will be able to sell all it wishes at the going price.

## Resource allocation

As we have seen earlier, every economy has somehow to 'decide' which goods and services to produce in which quantities and how the goods and services are to be produced. Thus, as goods and services are produced by the resources the economy possesses, 'decisions' have to be made about resource allocation. Further, the quantities of goods which people collectively would wish to consume will always be in excess of the quantities that the economy—with its endowments of land, labour, capital and know-how—will be able to produce. Thus they are scarce resources that have to be allocated.

We put 'decide' and 'decisions' in quotation marks as, under certain conditions, no set of decision-makers arrives at these decisions but the 'invisible hand' of the market leads to an allocation of resources that corresponds to the wishes of consumers. In modern economies such as Britain where—as we shall see in Chapter 7—a large proportion of employment and investment is under the control of the state, conscious decisions by governments are important. We shall also see in Chapter 6 that the prices of many goods are only in a very loose sense market-determined, since they are set by large companies. So in many senses the modern economy is far removed from the free market economy to which the analysis presented in earlier sections of this chapter is directly applicable.

It is important to understand the ways of the market, however, as the analysis is applicable to some sectors and can be modified to explain changes in allocation over time (we show this in the next chapter). Governments, too, have to decide how to allocate resources within the public sector, and some of the methods chosen have their roots in market allocation.

Let us take a pure market economy in which all productive units are small, in which the price of both goods and services is determined in the way described in the previous section, and in which the government plays no role in economic activity. Explanation is easiest if we describe an equilibrium configuration and then see what happens if this position is disturbed.

In equilibrium—the state in which no one has any incentive to change—the supply and demand of each good and service will be just matched at the current price. The typical firm in each industry will be earning a rate of profit which is just enough to keep it in that line of business. If profit were in excess of this then other firms would be attracted into that industry and the resulting increase in supply would reduce price and bring profit rates back to normal.

Firms, being profit maximisers, would employ the inputs necessary to produce in such combinations as to minimise costs of production. In the long run it is possible to produce goods using different factor combinations, i.e. employing, say, labour and machines in different proportions. Firms are assumed to choose between these alternative combinations on the basis of the relative prices of the two factors, these prices being themselves determined by supply and demand. It can be demonstrated that costs will be minimised if for any pair of factors the ratio of their marginal contributions to output (that is, how much output expands if the usage of the factor is increased by one unit, the usage of other factors remaining the same) is equal to the ratio of their prices. We can see intuitively why this is so. Say the marginal contribution of skilled labour is three times that of a unit of unskilled labour but that its price is only twice that of a unit of unskilled labour, and that it is possible for both skilled and unskilled labour to do the same tasks (the latter type simply takes longer). Then clearly the firm would gain more output for the same labour costs, or could get the same output at a lower cost, by employing more skilled labour and less unskilled.

Now let us take the case where in such an equilibrium position consumers' preferences change in such a way that they demand more electronic calculators. The demand curve for electronic calculators shifts upwards to the right and—as in Figure 8—the price rises. The increase in price induces extra electronic calculators to be produced; in the short run this extra output comes from working existing capacity more intensely by employing more labour or by inducing the existing labour force to work longer. Either way labour costs will rise, as to attract more labour from elsewhere the industry will have to offer higher wages, and similarly for extra hours of work. It is probable, however, that profits in the electronic calculator industry will become higher than normal and hence we have not yet arrived at a new long-run equilibrium. New firms will enter the industry and existing firms may expand capacity. As this occurs supply will increase further, driving price down from its short-run equilibrium level of $p_2$ (Figure 8). Whether the long-run level will be below or above the old level of $p_1$ we cannot say. (The answer depends on whether the industry is one in which long-run average costs rise, fall or stay constant as output expands. In a formal, mathematical, sense this model only works if all industries face constant long-run average costs—an assumption with little empirical foundation.) So in response to the increase in demand, the production of electronic calculators has risen and more men and machines are employed in their production. The extra resources were attracted into the industry by price incentives.

When consumers purchase more electronic calculators there will be a corresponding reduction in demand for other goods. The industries most affected will presumably be those producing substitutes for electronic calculators like logarithmic tables, mechanical calculators, abacuses and so on. Basically an inverse process will be at work here, with declining prices, output, wages and employment. Nor will these be the only industries affected. All firms supplying materials and components for electronic calculators will experience increases in demand and those supplying materials to the adversely affected substitute producers will experience declines in demand. Thus 'ripple' effects will spread through the economy.

It will no doubt occur to the reader that this adjustment process may take a long time, for there is no reason to suppose that the resources, particularly labour, released from the declining industries have the attributes required by those which expand.

That, then, is an outline of how the price mechanism, or the invisible hand of the market, operates. Of course, nobody pretends that in reality things could work as simply as this but there is a real division of opinion between those who believe that this sort of explanation is a reasonable approximation to reality and those who believe conditions in practice are so far from those assumed as to severely limit the applicability of this sort of treatment. Our position is that in some sectors of the economy things do work like this and that where they do not, an understanding of market forces is nonetheless useful. Some of the elements restricting the direct relevance of this sort of analysis are the existence of a large government sector, the fact that many prices are clearly not market-determined, the existence of monopolistic firms, the fact that relative wages do not seem to be determined by supply and demand and so on. We shall look further at these restrictions in the following three chapters.

## Commodity prices

Prices tend to be unstable in markets in which they are largely determined by supply and demand. This is especially true of commodity markets, and in this section we look briefly at commodity markets, particularly oil.

Figure 9 shows changes in the price of each raw material expressed in terms of changes in the price of manufactured goods. This is a rough and ready way in which to eliminate the effects of inflation. The relative price changes for many of these goods are very large.

Using simple supply and demand analysis we can see the causes of this price instability. In the years 1972–3 all the major industrial countries were experiencing a boom, largely caused by the huge Balance of Payments deficit run by the

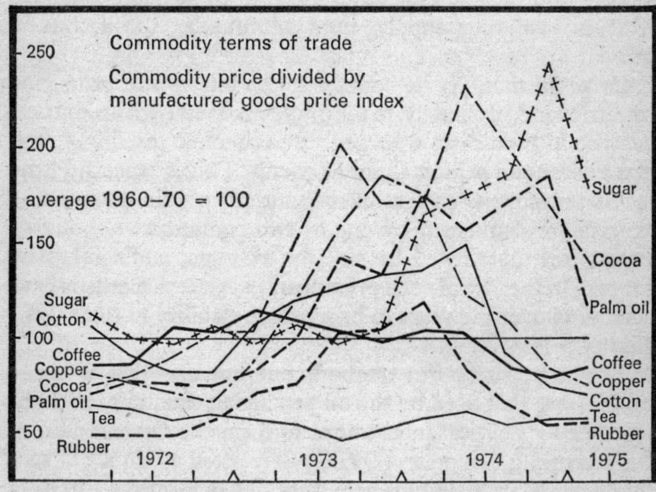


*Figure 9: Commodity terms of trade. The commodity price is divided by the manufactured goods price index*
*Source: The Economist*

United States. Hence the demand curves for most raw materials shifted to the right. This alone would cause prices to rise but most raw materials are in inelastic supply and hence the price changes were considerable. It is simply not possible for the output of say wool, sugar or copper to adjust quickly to a change in demand. So we had the world commodity price boom which ultimately caused inflation in industrial countries as the price of finished goods rose in consequence.

Industrial activity slackened off in 1973–4 when the oil producers combined to roughly treble their prices. As a result prices of commodities then fell dramatically. The extent of the fall in commodity prices will have been partially increased by the reaction of producers to the previous boom. Faced with high prices and increased demand some raw material producers attempted to increase their long-run capacity to produce—planting larger acreages, extending mines, reopening previously unprofitable mines etc. The fall in demand coincided with an increasing supply, thus accentuating the decline in prices.

Large fluctuations are counter to the interests of producing countries and, ultimately, to the interests of industrial countries, because in both cases they generate economic instability, and make corporate planning more difficult. This is especially true for those countries such as many South American states whose exports are dominated by one or two commodities. Bolivia's exports are dominated by tin, for example, and Chile's by copper. In the face of such price changes, various methods have been used over the years to bring some stability to some commodity prices.

The most successful method, but not one that is easily copied, was that used by the oil producing countries. Brought together by political motivations to form the Organisation of Oil Exporting Countries (OPEC) they acted as if they were a single producer, fixing his own price. They formed a *cartel*—a group of producers who jointly fix price and output. It is important to realise that output has to be controlled as well as price. For there is a world demand schedule for oil, which is very inelastic in the short run, and all that the OPEC countries can do is to choose whereabouts on it they want to be.

The pre-1973 price of oil was roughly \$3·30 a barrel. Assume that the market was roughly in equilibrium, so that supply equated with demand at that price. Even monopolists cannot fix both price and quantity, and when the price of oil was raised in 1973–4 to \$11 a barrel the total demand for OPEC oil declined. In fact, the decline in demand between its pre-embargo level in 1973 and mid-1975 was around 20%. We cannot use these figures to estimate the demand curve for oil, or the elasticity of demand for oil, as we cannot assume the demand curve for oil remained the same over this period. There is strong evidence that it was shifting to the left. The large increase in price led most western industrialised countries into a period of recession with falls in the level of national output. Curves relating demand to price are drawn on the assumption that income is constant; here, it was not. The high price of oil also stimulated investment in energy conservation and alternative forms of energy. So on all these counts the world demand curve for oil would have shifted to the left.

A cartel, to be successful, has to include all major producers or else outsiders will undercut their price, causing the latter to collapse. This condition was met by the OPEC cartel, where oil exports were concerned. But members of the cartel must agree on their objectives and on their price. In 1976 the interests of various members diverged: some wished to moderate price increases; others wanted relatively large price increases with consequent effects on output. Thus the cartel was coming under strain.

A method of price stabilisation which has been attempted in the case of some commodities since the war is to set up an agency to buy and sell the commodity. The detailed operation of such commodity agreements varies but in principle the agency sets a ceiling and a floor price. If the market price falls below the floor, then it buys on the open market and holds stocks which it then sells if the price reaches its ceiling. Clearly this can only be done in the case of non-perishable commodities—tin was an example. The floor and ceiling price has to be adjusted from time to time in line with underlying conditions but excessive price fluctuations can be avoided. The industrial countries showed little interest in such agreements up to 1970 but their experience then, when commodity prices increased by two and a half in three years has changed attitudes and we may see more attempts at price stabilisation in the future.

## The operation of markets

We conclude this chapter by examining markets where prices are not determined by supply and demand, and markets where the state intervenes to fix a price other than that which would otherwise rule.

Let us take the case where price is fixed by large suppliers. We think, for reasons that we shall explain in a subsequent chapter, that the pricing policy of most large firms is to add on a percentage mark up to average costs. Thus the price of Ford motor cars is determined by the Ford motor company and not

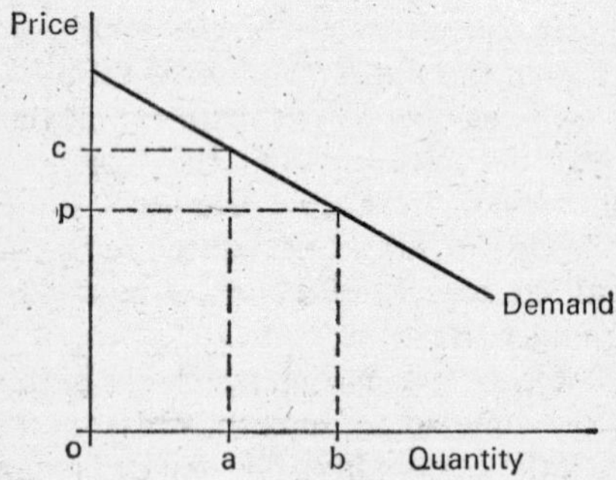


*Figure 10*

by the operation of the forces of supply and demand. Which is not to say that these forces have no relevance. What in effect happens is that Ford fix the price of a model and the market then determines how many cars are sold at that price. The company then adjusts output in line. Thus, in this case, instead of price being the adjustment mechanism, output is.

This may lead to odd situations. The Jaguar XJ12, for example, was originally priced at a level considerably below that which would rule in a competitive market. The situation can be depicted diagrammatically, as in Figure 10.

The company could supply *oa* units per period but at the price fixed *op*, *ob* units per week were demanded. In a competitive market the price would have increased to *oc*. Here, however, the price of the XJ12 was fixed by Jaguar at *op*. Three things happened. First long waiting lists for the car developed. Second, as there is no price-fixing in the market for second-hand cars, people lucky enough to obtain one could promptly resell it at a profit. Third, payments—bribes—to retailers were made in order to obtain such cars. The behaviour of the company was not completely irrational, for it could slowly adjust supply upwards and it could ensure a demand for the car for several years. It did in fact subsequently adjust the price.

We see again the development of secondary markets in the case of tickets for the Cup Final and other major sporting occasions. The Football Association fixes the price of Cup Final tickets below the equilibrium level with the result that some of the supply gets into the hands of touts who can sell the tickets at a profit. Again, although the Football Association is not maximising its short-run profits it is not acting irrationally. For if very high prices were charged this might alienate regular supporters, to the detriment of sales for other matches.

Governments often fix prices at levels other than those which would obtain in a free market. The price of rented unfurnished accommodation is an example. For a long time now successive governments have, by various means, controlled rents. By setting rents below market levels they have reduced the supply of such accommodation and have created a permanent situation of excess demand. In the face of this the only way out has been for the government itself to provide such accommodation in the form of local authority housing.

Where prices are fixed at levels other than those which could rule in the market—either for social, commercial or other reasons—then some adjustment has to be made. This can take the form of queues, the development of black markets, and many other forms. But although supply and demand analysis can be misleading, and although many prices are not established in this way, the concepts involved are fundamental.

FURTHER READING

R. Turvey's *Supply and Demand* (Allen and Unwin, 1971) covers the basic analysis and contains many case-studies.

# 6

# The Firm

## Introduction

In discussing the market in the previous chapter we were at pains to emphasise that in its simple form the analysis only applied to markets dominated by small firms. Here, therefore, we turn to a discussion of large firms which in all industrial economies account for a large amount of total output, especially in manufacturing. In Britain in 1968 the fifty largest firms accounted for 32% of total manufacturing output and 29% of total employment in manufacturing. The corresponding shares of the two hundred largest firms were 53% and 47% respectively.

Large firms are not spread widely either across the whole economy or within manufacturing and one of the questions with which we shall be concerned is why the size of the firm varies between sectors. In manufacturing, large firms tend to dominate the chemical and petroleum industries, tobacco and motor vehicles, while in clothing, textiles and printing the share of output taken by the largest firm is relatively low. In the service sector the typical unit is small but large units again account for a large proportion of turnover. In retailing, for example, 95% of all organisations have only one establishment and collectively are responsible for just under a half of retail turnover: on the other hand about 0·3% of all organisations have over ten establishments, but these account for about 30% of total retail turnover.

## Market structures

Economists have devised a classification of markets according to the number and characteristics of constituent firms and it will help to fix ideas if we briefly run through some of the more important of these market structures.

One extreme form of market structure is known as *perfect competition*, much beloved by economic theorists. In perfectly competitive markets all firms are small, act independently of each other, and as each firm will account for a small fraction of the output of the industry it has no control over price. There are no obstacles to entry to such industries. Some markets will approximate to this, particularly, as we argued in Chapter 5, the markets for some commodities, although even here collusion and government interference are fairly common.

In perfectly competitive markets, prices are determined by supply and demand as outlined in the previous chapter. Each firm will tend to earn a normal or average rate of profit. Should price settle at a level which gives profits higher than those being earned in other industries with a similar degree of risk, then new firms will tend to enter the industry, expanding supply and driving down prices.

The other extreme—and perhaps even more rare—is pure *monopoly*. Here the total output of a good is controlled by a single producer. To make operational sense of this structure it has to be extended to cover situations where although there may be more than one producer the largest is so large that it can ignore the rest and act as if it were a pure monopolist. One of the closest approximations to a pure monopolist is the British Oxygen Company, about which the Monopolies Commission has had some harsh words to say.

To preserve a monopoly position a firm must be able to prevent others entering the industry or to prevent peripheral firms from attaining a significant market share. There must be barriers to entry. These may be legal as in the case of patents—British Nylon Spinners had a legal monopoly from 1940–56—but are more usually financial in the sense that the initial costs of entering a monopolistic market are very high. These costs may take the form of capital equipment, of advertising, or of securing adequate distributive channels. There is nothing, then, to prevent a monopolist from earning excess profits, for potential competitors are barred. Monopolists will tend to have, for any given level of costs, higher prices and consequently lower outputs than would obtain if competition took place. It is important to remember that monopolists cannot fix both prices and the quantity they sell: once price is fixed, market demand determines how much is bought.

Most market forms in practice lie between the extremes of perfect competition and monopoly but can be defined with respect to the characteristics of these two sorts of market. Thus, once we allow for product differentiation, every producer will have an element of monopoly, for he is the only seller of his brand of the product. The more he can convince consumers by packaging and advertising that his brand is different from other brands of the same good, the greater will be his degree of monopoly and the greater his control over the price he charges. The situation where there are a fairly large number of producers of branded goods is referred to as *imperfect competition* or *monopolistic competition*, the titles reflecting the elements of monopoly and of competition that occur in such markets. Industries where the market share of the three or four largest firms is relatively small—say less than 40%—could be described as imperfectly competitive.

As a final case we will consider *oligopoly*, a situation where there are few producers. The essential characteristic of oligopoly is interdependence between producers rather than a small number of producers. In oligopoly no firm is so large that it can ignore the others, no firm so small that the others can ignore it. Once again pure oligopoly will be almost impossible to find because there will almost always be a fringe of small firms. Thus the definition of interdependence should be interpreted as referring to the largest firms, ignoring the periphery. An important feature of oligopoly is the absence of price competition. This is a result of interdependence. If one firm is considering increasing price it will consider that the most likely reaction of its competitors will be to leave their prices unchanged. It will therefore expect to lose sales. If, on the other hand, it is considering a price reduction it will expect the others to follow its price cut and that it will end up with roughly the same sales volume at a lower price. Thus nothing much is to be gained by raising or lowering prices relative to those charged by the other firms. Prices have to be raised when costs rise, however, and in many oligopolistic industries there is an informal system of price leadership. If one firm raises prices in line with cost increases which are experienced by the others then the price change will be followed. Examples of oligopolistic industries where all firms change their prices more or less simultaneously are tobacco, petrol and banking. Competition in oligopoly has thus to take non-price forms; large scale advertising, sponsored competitions, offers, unlovely free goods and all the paraphernalia of marketing are common in oligopolistic industries and therefore in virtually all Western industrial societies.

*Table 6*

*Concentration in British Manufacturing Industry 1968*

| *Five-firm concentration ratio* | *Number of industries* |
|---|---|
| 0–10 | 0 |
| 10–30 | 28 |
| 30–50 | 61 |
| 50–70 | 80 |
| 70–90 | 85 |
| 90–100 | 70 |

*Source: S. Aaronovitch and M. Sawyer: Lloyds Bank Review, 1974.*

Some idea of the number of industries which are dominated by a few firms can be gained from figures on industrial concentration. The five-firm concentration ratio, the measure used in Table 6, shows the share of sales taken by the five largest firms.

In about half of the industries the five largest firms accounted for over 70% of sales. In the most concentrated industries the largest firm must have had at least 18% of total sales, and almost certainly more. This shows one of the weaknesses of concentration ratios as an indicator of market structure—we do not know how the sales are distributed between the five largest firms. We can conclude that over half of manufacturing industries, which also account for about a half of sales in manufacturing, are oligopolistic or monopolistic. In a later section we will examine the reasons for this, but first we discuss the motives and objectives of companies.

## The objectives of firms

In order to be able to say much about the behaviour of firms we need to know what it is that firms are trying to do; we need to know their objectives. For a long time the view was that firms try to maximise their profits but in recent decades various alternative objectives have been suggested which give rise to various theories of the firm.

In traditional theory firms try to maximise profits. This has an obvious intuitive appeal and is also symmetrical with the supposed behaviour of consumers. Consumers, as we have seen, are supposed to maximise the utility or satisfaction they derive from their expenditure and it seems reasonable that producers maximise their rewards, which take the form of profit. On the basis of these twin maximisation behaviours it is possible, as we saw in the previous chapter, to erect an elegant theory which shows that, left to their own devices, consumers and producers will bring about an allocation of resources which is optimal in the sense that society will maximise its economic welfare.

To state that firms maximise profits is not very helpful unless the period of time over which profits are to be maximised is specified. By setting the price which maximises this period's profits, a firm may sacrifice some of next period's profits and we have seen that, in order to ensure future profits, firms often charge prices lower than the market will bear. The problem is that if long-term profit maximisation is held to be the aim of the firm it is difficult to predict its price and output behaviour in any given short period. Leaving that aside it seems reasonable to suppose that when firms are owned by an individual, profits will be his primary objective.

The major attack on the theory of profit maximisation stemmed from the increasing divorce of ownership from control in the large company. The owners of a company are the shareholders and experience has shown that they are unlikely to interfere in the running of the firm as long as reasonable dividends are paid and/or a reasonable rate of growth of the share price is maintained. Nowadays, many shareholders are institutions, particularly insurance companies and pension funds, and the managers of these institutions have shown themselves to be even less willing to exert their power than are private individuals. As a result, shareholders' meetings are invariably poorly attended with the accounts and the company report usually being accepted without question. Thus the company is actually run by paid managers who may have no shares in the company or only a nominal holding. As the managers do not receive the profits, it is argued, why should they seek to maximise them?

So if managers do not seek maximum profit what is it that they are trying to do? One of the first propositions, put forward by W. J. Baumol in 1959, was that managers are primarily interested in sales or turnover. The status of a manager is judged by the size of the firm he works for rather than by its profits. Thus the maximisation of sales revenue is an alternative theory of corporate behaviour. Profits still enter the picture, for if in the pursuit of sales revenue the level of profit falls below that earned elsewhere the shareholders will cease to be acquiescent and may dismiss the managers. Subject to this limitation the maximisation of sales revenue is held to be the major objective of large companies.

A variant of this theory is that the objective is the rate of growth of sales. Here profits act on the one hand as a constraint (enough must be earned to keep shareholders happy) and on the other as a means of continuing growth (most investment is financed out of undistributed profits).

If we continue the line of thought that managers try to achieve what gives them satisfaction—in the above case, sales—we arrive at more general 'managerial' theories of the firm. Here we list a series of things which give managers utility and propose that in some way it is managerial utility that is maximised. There is one set of items, collectively termed 'managerial slack', which is normally included. Managerial slack consists of things which managers like but which are not essential to the organisation of the firm. Examples are pretty secretaries rather than plain ones, larger cars rather than small, lavish expense accounts and so on. As well as managerial slack it is often assumed that managers like to have a large number of staff responsible to them and to have discretionary control over investment. Whatever we include, the level of profits will always enter as a constraint upon managerial discretion. This all seems very reasonable but the danger is that the theory becomes so general as to be useless in predicting corporate behaviour.

There are other theories of corporate behaviour but we have done enough in this brief summary to indicate the difficulty of analysing company objectives. It is safe to say that no single theory will suffice and that there will be some firms who happen to have profit as a high priority, others who aim at large sales and so on.

## The advantages of scale

We have seen that in some industries output is spread between a large number of smallish firms whereas in others the major part of output is produced by a few firms. In sketching the reason for this diversity we will initially continue to confine our attention to manufacturing industry.

Technology provides part of the answer. The size of plant that will give the minimum production costs per unit will vary from industry to industry. In oil refining, steel production and car assembly, to mention only a few, the technical conditions of production are such that large plants will be able to produce at significantly lower cost than will small plants. In other industries, spinning and weaving of textiles for example, the optimum size of productive unit is small, with large plants being at a disadvantage. This does not exhaust the list of possibilities. There will be industries where costs per unit are roughly the same whatever the size of plant; the production of cigarettes is thought to be an example of such an industry. Here large and small plants can co-exist. There is some evidence that in the brewing industry there are two optimum sizes of brewery—one fairly small (employing around 200 men), one very large. Such technical influences will only determine the size of plant. Although this may be correlated with the size of the firm, to explain fully the size of multi-plant firms we have to look further. Large firms reap benefits in the marketing and financial aspects of their operation. Large buyers usually buy on relatively favourable terms and there often exist economies of scale in selling. Marketing organisations have a minimum effective size and as sales rise, unit costs of selling decline. Scale economies may exist in advertising. An American study has shown that although General Motors spent as much on advertising as the rest of the USA motor industry put together, its advertising costs per car sold were lower than those of any of its competitors. Large units are also able to obtain loan and equity finance more easily and on cheaper terms.

Up to a certain point there also exist managerial advantages of size. The large firm can employ specialists in the various aspects of management and organisation whereas in small firms managers have to turn their hand to several tasks. Beyond some point, however, the managerial problems are more likely to act as a constraint. Large organisations of any sort are difficult to organise and manage, managerial talent is scarce and management science is a young and undeveloped discipline. Refuge is often sought in bureaucracy and red tape and it may be difficult to make decisions quickly. One currently fashionable way out of this problem is to decentralise the decision-making process but co-ordination is then made that much more difficult.

A further advantage that is often claimed for the large firm is that it is more likely to devote a relatively high proportion of its resources to research and development activities and to secure a faster rate of innovation. As the rate of innovation is likely to be a key determinant of the rate of economic growth, the validity or otherwise of this claim is of some importance. A survey of the evidence led to the conclusion that although medium-sized and large firms were more likely to undertake research and development than small firms it was not true that very large firms spent more proportionately on these activities than did large and medium-sized firms.

There exist, then, various economies of scale from which

large firms can benefit. Their incidence will vary from industry to industry and this largely explains why, in some manufacturing industries the average size of firm is small and in others it is large. Similar influences are at work in the service sector of the economy. Here the typical unit is much smaller than in manufacturing although, as we have seen, large units often account for a disproportionate share of turnover. Production of personal services has, by definition, to be located at the point of sale and this will keep the size of unit small. Hairdressing is a classic example of a trade where there appear to be few advantages of size and where the typical unit is small.

Other motives for growth should be obvious from our previous discussion. In so far as managers derive satisfaction from running large units they will strive to enlarge the size of the firm. Large firms will have greater control over their price, will be less exposed to competition and will tend to have more stable output patterns than small firms. Whether the social advantages of large units outweigh the disadvantages associated with a restriction of competition is of crucial importance for government industrial policy and we return to this in the final section of this chapter.

## Pricing

We have seen that the production of some goods and services takes place under competitive conditions and that the market structure may correspond in a rough and ready way to perfect competition. Here prices will be determined by supply and demand in the way outlined in the previous chapter. Producers will largely be price takers and they then decide whether, and how much, to sell at the market price. In most of manufacturing and in some parts of the service sector oligopoly and restricted competition are the rule. How do these firms set their prices?

From the empirical evidence there seems little doubt that mark-up or full cost pricing is typical. The firm estimates the average cost of producing the good and then adds on a percentage mark-up for profit. This seems straightforward but there are two issues to be settled—for what level of output are average costs estimated, and how is the mark-up determined?

Average costs of production are total costs divided by the number of units produced. Average costs will vary with output mainly, but not entirely, because as output is expanded within a plant of a given size the fixed costs of the plant and administration are spread over more and more units of output. Most plants will produce more than one product so some method has to be found of allocating overhead costs between the different products. This is an accounting problem. Our question is, for which level of output are average costs calculated for this purpose? The answer seems to be that 'normal' output is used: this will vary from industry to industry but might roughly be taken as about 80–90% of the maximum possible capacity of the plant. The evidence shows that this is adhered to throughout the trade cycle. Thus when demand is low and average costs are higher than normal (as fixed costs are spread across fewer units of output) the actual profit margin falls and vice versa when the plant is working at capacity.

The second question is what determines the mark-up? It is this aspect of the mark-up hypothesis as a theory of pricing that its opponents have attacked. Presumably the mark-up will be greater the less the amount of competition and the greater is the degree of uncertainty. As far as predicting price behaviour in an industry is concerned, this lack of a coherent explanation of the mark-up is not a problem as long as some normal mark-up exists. Mark-ups change, however. We will see in Chapter 8 that it seems as though mark-ups in British industry declined in the 1960s.

We can now use this theory of pricing to show how relative prices change over time and thus complete the discussion of resource allocation that we began in the previous chapter. The starting point is technological change, which can take the form of new or better products or of cheaper methods of production. We usually measure technological change by the rate of growth of output per man and on this basis the rate of technological change varies significantly across industries, tending to be greatest in science-based industries like chemicals and electronics and lowest in service industries. Wages, however, as we shall see in Chapter 8, increase by very similar amounts in each industry. Suppose this rate of increase of wages in one year is 8%; then in an industry where output per man has also increased by 8% firms will face unchanged *unit* costs and will therefore, on the mark-up hypothesis, leave prices unaltered. A low productivity growth industry, however, will have to increase its prices. If output per man increases by 2% while wages go up by 8%, then to maintain mark-ups, prices must rise by 6%. It is very rare to see the price of a manufactured good decline (although electronic industries in the mid-1970s would be an exception) but we can see how *relative* prices change even in the absence of downward price flexibility. From the theory of demand outlined in the last chapter we would expect the demand for products whose relative prices fall to increase, the extent of the increase depending on the price elasticity of demand. Thus some industries will grow faster than others.

There is another important influence at work. Real incomes increase in line with the growth of national productivity (say 2–3% a year in the United Kingdom) and as we have seen, the income elasticity of demand is high for the products of some industries and low for those of others. Normally in industrial economies the income elasticity of demand for the products of service industries is high, but these tend to be products whose relative price increases over time because of a low rate of productivity growth. Thus the two influences (price changes and changes in income) may often work in different directions and the outcome is uncertain. The point is, however, that changes in resource allocation will follow from the net result of these influences.

## Government monopolies and mergers policy

The importance of large firms in the economy has been increasing in recent decades. One way of illustrating this in manufacturing industry is to examine the share of output claimed by the largest firms.

*Table 7*

*Shares of largest firms in output of manufacturing industry*

| | *1935* | *1958* | *1963* | *1968* |
|---|---|---|---|---|
| Largest 50 firms | 14·9 | 24·7 | 27·9 | 32·4 |
| Largest 200 firms | — | 41·0 | 47·9 | 52·4 |

*Source: As Table 6*

There is no doubt that concentration has also been increasing in the non-manufacturing sectors of the economy. The growth in concentration can come about either through the internal expansion of individual firms or through mergers. Recent work suggests that these two factors were of equal importance in the increase in industrial concentration since the war.

The level of merger activity in Britain has been particularly high since the mid-1960s and this trend has been evident in a number of other industrial countries, particularly in West Germany and in the United States. The basic reason for this merger activity has been to gain the advantages of size that we discussed previously, which is not to say that these advantages have necessarily been realised. There are very great problems in comparing firms before and after growth but, as it stands, what little research there is suggests that the results of growth by merger are significantly inferior to those of growth through internal expansion.

Whatever the mechanism of growth the fact remains that large units dominate much of industry—the two hundred largest firms account for over one half of manufacturing output—and are doing so to an increasing extent. What is the attitude of government to large firms and to collusion between firms? Legislation on this matter in Britain dates from 1948 and can conveniently be considered in three parts—policy towards monopolies and mergers, towards resale price maintenance and towards restrictive practices.

In its policy towards *monopolies and mergers* the government has tried to balance the advantages and disadvantages of large firms. Monopolies have not been judged as harmful *per se* but only where the social disadvantages have been found to outweigh the advantages; in fact some agencies have been established with the aim of promoting desirable mergers. We have already outlined these advantages and disadvantages. Large firms often achieve lower unit costs of production but on the other hand may charge higher prices and earn higher profits than would obtain in a competitive environment. Under British legislation a firm is defined as holding a monopoly position if it controls 25% of the market for a good. This figure has no basis in any economic theory—nor would any other figure—but some definition of monopoly has, of course, to be chosen. The Monopolies Commission has had the task of investigating cases referred to it by the government or lately by the Director of Fair Trading. It has found it extraordinarily difficult to assess whether a monopoly position is being abused and has found it impossible to come up with a set of criteria to apply to all cases. Even in the relatively few cases where the Commission has reported strongly against a company, the strongest action taken by the government has been to secure undertakings about its future operation from the company. It is, of course, very difficult to break up a company once it is established, and recognition of this led to the 1965 act which gave the government power to refer proposed mergers to the Commission. In these cases the Commission has to report quickly and is unable to undertake the exhaustive enquiries which characterise its monopoly references.

On *restrictive practices*, such as price or market-sharing agreements between firms, the policy has been much clearer. There is rarely any countervailing advantage to set against the restriction of competition and since the 1956 act which required restrictive practices to be registered, most formal agreements have been abandoned. It seems fairly clear, however, that in many cases tacit understandings have replaced formal agreements, leaving the real situation unaltered.

The final part of the policy was the ending in 1964 of *resale price maintenance*—the right of a manufacturer to fix the retail price of his good. This brought a wave of competition into retailing which has conferred substantial benefits upon consumers.

We conclude by making a brief reference to one particular type of large firm which some have thought to be potentially dangerous—the multinational enterprise. A *multinational* enterprise is one which has productive capacity in more than one country. Although this need not imply that such firms are large, they usually are. A few figures will show this. Collectively multinationals account for no less than a fifth of world output (excluding the eastern bloc). Their liquid assets are twice the amount of the world's gold and exchange reserves; if the size of nations is measured by national income and the size of multinationals by their gross sales, then of the 100 largest units in the world, 40 are multinationals, 60 are countries. Their relative importance is increasing—in recent years the output of multinationals has been growing at about twice the rate of world output.

The main objections that have been levied against multinationals are threefold. There is first the nationalistic argument that it is dangerous to allow control over a significant proportion of national resources to be in the hands of foreigners. Second, multinationals are interested in minimising their tax burden, and by setting artificial transfer prices between units located in different countries they can report the bulk of their profits where taxes are low. This has two disadvantages for host countries: it reduces tax revenues and the prices charged by multinationals need not reflect underlying cost and demand conditions and can lead to a misallocation of resources. Third, it is possible that these companies may be able to respond differently to policy measures than do national firms and that they may thus thwart domestic government policy. The extent to which this is presently true is not clear, but if it proves to be a problem the answer will have to be the establishment of supra-national government organisations.

FURTHER READING

J. Galbraith's *American Capitalism* (Pelican, 1963) is an interesting view of large corporations.

# 7

# The Public Sector

## The extent of the public sector

A hundred years ago the public sector consisted of the army and navy, the Post Office and a few rotten boroughs. Nowadays, it embraces a great variety of institutions which are loosely organised as a whole. At the centre is the state itself: Parliament, the Cabinet, and its direct offshoots, the government departments. Some departments are relatively small, like the Ministry of Agriculture, Fisheries and Food; others, like the Department of the Environment, are extremely big. Some departments run large enterprises—for example, the National Health Service, sometimes described as the tenth biggest corporation in the world. Then there are the state boards, public corporations and major nationalised industries—the Post Office, the fuel and power industries, steel, transport, aerospace and shipbuilding, and a series of firms of which the state is wholly or in part the owner. And beyond this complex of nationalised and semi-nationalised concerns is a series of subsidised activities, like the Royal Opera House, which operate wholly or in part with public money. The central government part of the public sector, then, is extensive and heterogeneous.

The local government sector is also large but it is more homogeneous than that of central government. It consists of environmental services (like roads, parks, cemeteries), social services, housing and education. These services, though limited in number, are substantial. The education service, for example, employs about one and a half million people full- and part-time, while local authorities own over a third of all houses and flats.

The public sector is not easy to define exactly and giving precise statistics about its magnitude poses problems, but we can give a rough indication of its relative size in various ways, as shown in Tables 8, 9 and 10.

*Table 8*

*Number of Employees in the Public Sector*

| | *June 1963* Thousands | % of total | *June 1974* Thousands | % of total |
|---|---|---|---|---|
| Total employed UK labour force | 24 663 | | 25 112 | |
| *Public sector:* | **5 914** | **24·0** | **6 843** | **27·2** |
| Central government | 1 770 | 7·2 | 2 069 | 8·2 |
| Local authorities | 2 008 | 8·1 | 2 844 | 11·3 |
| Public corporations | 2 136 | 8·7 | 1 930 | 7·7 |

*Source: P. 123, Economic Trends, February 1976*

*Table 9*

*Gross Domestic Fixed Capital Formation by Sector (millions of pounds)*

| | *Total* | *Private* | *Public* | |
|---|---|---|---|---|
| 1965 | 6 504 | 3 724 | 2 780 | (42·8%) |
| 1975 | 20 510 | 11 697 | 8 813 | (42·6%) |

*Source: National Income and Expenditure 1965–75 (HMSO 1975)*

*Table 10*

*Current Expenditure on Goods and Services by the Public Sector (millions of pounds)*

| | *1965* | *1975* |
|---|---|---|
| Consumption | 6 041 | 22 907 |
| Investment | 2 781 | 8 813 |
| **Total** | **8 822** | **31 720** |
| As percentage of Gross National Product | (31 656) | (94 095) |
| | 27·9% | 33·7% |

*Source: National Income and Expenditure 1965–75.*

It should be noted, however, that the tax/transfer system means that a higher proportion of the GNP than that shown in Table 10 passes through government hands.

The notion that one person, the Prime Minister, or twenty or so men and women in the Cabinet, can 'control' so large a public sector is manifestly absurd if by 'control' is meant detailed daily supervision. If they each gave a thousand orders for something to be done each year, it would take a thousand years for every public servant to be told once what to do. So the system—and it is only a 'system' by convenience of language—is run by rules and conventions. Interestingly enough, despite differences in political philosophy and social history between—say—the United States, Sweden, Great Britain and Germany, the size and scope of the public sector does not differ widely from country to country at a given level of economic development. Broadly speaking each country has a public social security, health and education system of similar size. The differences occur in the extent of public ownership of basic and manufacturing industries. In most countries fuel and power are nationalised; in France, half the car-making industry; in Italy a whole range of firms; but in Germany and the United States this is not so—though even there the boundaries between the private and public sectors are indistinct (the US aerospace industry, for instance, has been largely dependent upon orders from the Defence Department).

## Why there is a large public sector

There are three reasons why the public sector is the size that it is. The first is that it just happened, as the result of wars—the First and Second World Wars and the cold war greatly enlarged governmental activity; as the result of pressure for the welfare state; and because when various parts of the public sector (like the telephone system in most countries) happen to fall into the hands of the state they are rarely returned to the private sector. Accident plays a major part in life; it needs no theory of sinister conspiracy to explain where we are.

The second explanation of the size of the public sector is political. It has been a tenet of one major branch of socialist thought that the elimination of the profit motive and of the receipt of profits is a necessary condition of the creation of the good society. 'Production for use, not for profit' is a very powerful slogan. Thus it has been a strong argument for the public ownership of the means of production, distribution and exchange, that such a change of ownership from private to public hands was a necessary condition of a society with an equitable distribution of income and a satisfactory set of working conditions. Consequently shifts of the boundary between the public and private sectors have been associated with the election of left-wing governments. But this has not necessarily been associated with public ownership of industry. Sweden, which has the largest proportionate public sector in the OECD, has achieved it by the expansion of welfare services, not by the nationalisation of firms, while countries like Spain have fairly large public sectors but limited social services.

There is a third reason for public ownership, which is a matter of pure economic theory. There are some goods and services which possess to some degree the characteristics of what are termed *public goods*. The degree to which a good is 'public' can be measured in two dimensions—the extent to which it is 'non-rival' and the extent to which it is 'non-excludable' (the terms are those of Professor Musgrave). A good is non-rival if its enjoyment by one person does not diminish the amount available for others to enjoy. An example would be a TV programme, once transmitted. The fact that I am watching does not reduce the amount available for you. Most goods do not, of course, possess this characteristic; if I purchase a car then the resources used to produce the car are not available to anyone else. A good is 'non-excludable' if it is impossible to exclude people from benefiting from its provision. Virtually the only examples are national defence and lighthouses. To take the latter, once a lighthouse is flashing its signal it is available, free, to anyone within sight. Because so few goods qualify under this second characteristic it really has to be modified to include goods—like rural roads, for which it would be extremely expensive—even if technically possible—to charge.

In any event the 'theory' of public goods is of minimal practical interest. In practice public goods are best taken as being those that governments normally feel it their duty to provide. In the case of pure public goods it is obvious that the government has to provide them, for no one else will, as it is not possible to charge the beneficiaries. Nor will any one beneficiary have any incentive to offer to pay, for he knows that, as long as someone induces a supply, he will be bound to benefit. In the case of many of the goods the government chooses to provide, in practice the main justification is that it is probable that people by themselves would buy less than is desirable in the public interest. An example would be health care. In the absence of a state health service, when a member of the labour force is ill, he imposes costs on himself (the cost of treatment and of the income he forgoes through not working) and on others (his absence may disrupt work schedules, cause a train not to run, or a lecture not to be given). In deciding how much health care to purchase (or to insure for) he will only take into account the costs that he himself will bear and thus the amount of health care provided will be less than is socially optimal. It is probable that education is a similar sort of good. Goods whose consumption, or production, imposes benefits on others which do not have to be paid for are said to generate external benefits. We will discuss this further below.

## The allocation of resources in the public sector

Once the public provision of some goods is decided upon, the central question is: what should determine the allocation of public resources? If a good or service is needed by the community, somebody has to decide how much is needed, and who shall have it. In the case of many things this is done in the way that it is done by private enterprise. We pay a price for telephones, for posting letters, for gas and electricity. Of course public corporations may make losses, and so subsidise their customers, but that is incidental. A subsidy can be given to commodities produced by private enterprise, too, like food. But some services are provided free to those who directly benefit from them—parks, roads, education, medical care—and their cost is levied on the general body of taxpayers. There is, of course, no such thing as a genuinely 'free' good, except air, because everything requires effort to produce it.

The terms on which these goods and services are allocated to the public vary. Most people do not use all of the services all of the time—that is, demand is not unlimited. If everybody used the parks 24 hours a day they would look like refugee camps. So access to public facilities is limited—the schools are available for certain age-groups, and access to hospitals is determined by medical priority. A queue of patients is formed, and the less keen patients cure themselves, seek treatment elsewhere or die before they are admitted. This rationing of public facilities substitutes professional judgement for individual judgement. It is not possible to go to a state school and say 'teach me Greek at once', or to a doctor and say 'cut my leg off'. To do the first you have to go to a private crammer, and few doctors would be willing to do the second. There is a heated political argument between those who regard access to health and education on these terms as part of an authoritarian and paternalistic development of society, and those who regard the provision of services free of charge at point of access as a necessary condition of the good society, enabling professional care to be given when it is required, free of the taint of money. Economics has tended to favour the first view; perhaps because economics is itself politically tainted.

The economics of the public sector are best considered apart from those goods and services like gas and electricity that are provided at a price like the products of private business. If we think of the 'free' sector—that is, those goods and services that are provided to the consumer free of charge or at a very greatly reduced price—we have to decide on what principle the amount and quality of the service is determined. Suppose we look at Table 11 which analyses public expenditure in various fields in 1958 and 1975. (Transfer payments are included; total expenditure thus exceeds that of Table 10.)

*Table 11*

*Public Expenditure in the UK*
*(millions of pounds)*

| | *1958* | *% of total* | *1975* | *% of total* |
|---|---|---|---|---|
| **Total public expenditure (excluding debt interest)** | **7 262** | | **49 952** | |
| Military and civil defence | 1 545 | 21·3 | 5 189 | 10·4 |
| Education | 786 | 10·8 | 6 840 | 13·7 |
| National Health Service | 728 | 10·0 | 5 260 | 10·5 |
| Social Security benefits | 1 345 | 18·5 | 8 918 | 17·9 |
| Housing and the environment | 698 | 9·6 | 6 696 | 13·4 |
| Industry and trade | 522 | 7·2 | 5 285 | 10·6 |

*Source: Table 346, Annual Abstract of Statistics, 1976.*

We see that the allocation between different areas has altered over the years. This is the result of the political process. For many years now the immediate threat of a major war has seemed to diminish, so defence expenditure has relatively (but not absolutely) fallen. With improving living standards, and a birth-rate that rose until 1964, the demand for education has been increasing at all levels. The same is true for housing. All these pressures are indicated through the political process. A threat by Scotland to leave the United Kingdom leads to greater public expenditure in Scotland. A powerful minister of transport leads to extra road-building.

It is tempting for non-political persons to describe these decisions on expenditure as 'non-economic' or even 'irrational'. But it is by no means obvious that a decision on the part of millions to eat cornflakes rather than porridge for breakfast is more rational than a political debate about whether health comes before or after education.

## Allocative techniques

The decision to allocate resources between different services like education, health and defence is essentially a matter of history modified by politics. At any point in time the adjustments are marginal—one more aircraft carrier, 100 fewer schools—and only occasionally are public services totally uprooted. These major decisions are bound to be the result of long-term public pressure and public debate. But within a particular service—say, education—there is a major problem which is both economic and political. How are resources to be allocated between different parts of the sector? Suppose, for example, that it is agreed that more should be spent on defence. Should it go to the army, the navy or the air force? Again, there are political pressures, and there is an hereditary burden of expenditure which can only be gradually changed.

There are really two great issues. One is that resources are allocated by particular functions—for example, the army, the navy or the air force—and these functions are sources of independent power. But the problems that the resources have to deal with go across particular functions. Thus the problem, for example, of childhood deprivation involves social security, housing, education and health. There is a real difficulty in allocating resources to achieve the ends that people want, difficulties which are both conceptual and practical.

One popular economic technique for allocating resources is *cost benefit analysis*. This is a technique whereby the total costs of a particular course of action are added up, whether they are borne by a public agency, a private firm or an individual, and subtracted from the total benefits, similarly calculated, to give a figure for the net value of the project. For example, a child care programme would include the costs of medical and education programmes provided by the state, private charity, and expenditure by the parents. In a Chinese commune or an Israeli kibbutz, for example, where all parents work, somebody has to be paid to look after the very small children whereas, generally speaking, in OECD countries the mother does so without charge to the community. This example also illustrates one of the problems with cost benefit analysis—the benefits of a child care programme are very difficult to calculate quantitatively.

A cost benefit exercise is, in principle, the same as the investment calculations undertaken by firms, although as we will see shortly there are two important differences. One problem common to both is that the costs will usually occur mainly in the short run while, for example, a road is being built, whereas the benefit stream will accrue in the future. Sums receivable today are, however, worth less than sums receivable in the future, and hence some adjustment has to be made to bring them up to a common basis.

Let us first remind the reader why a sum of money receivable now is worth more than the same sum receivable in a year's time. It is a matter of compound interest. If I have £100 now and the interest rate is 10% then this will grow to £110 in one year's time. Therefore £100 receivable in one year's time has a *present value* of £$\frac{100}{110}$ now, or £90·9. Similarly £100 lent for two years at 10% compound interest will grow to £121 in two years. Thus £100 receivable in two year's time has a present value of £82·6. The technique of reducing the benefit of sums receivable or the burden of costs incurred in the future is known as *discounting*. The rate at which future sums are reduced (discounted) is known as the discount rate. There is an enormous literature on how the discount rate to be used in public investment appraisal should be determined, but in practice the rate used seems to approximate to the long-term interest rate. Because resources now are worth more than resources in the future, these flows of costs and benefits have to be brought back to current values so that they can be compared. This process has nothing to do with inflation, however, as in an investment appraisal all future costs and benefits are valued at today's prices: it is, as we said, a matter of compound interest.

Cost benefit analysis for the public sector differs from the investment appraisal undertaken by private firms in two important respects. First all the costs and benefits are included, irrespective of who pays or receives them. In other words external benefits and costs are included. In private appraisals only those costs and returns accruing to the firm in question are included. Thus a project which a firm would not undertake may be found worth while in the public sector and vice versa.

One of the earliest cost benefit studies in this country was that carried out for the Victoria tube line in London. This was published in 1963 which serves to illustrate how recently this technique has been developed. Many of the benefits of the Line accrue to road users in the form of savings in time from reduced traffic congestion and these outweighed the benefits to users of the Line. The fares levied would not cover the costs of the Victoria Line—hence no private undertaking would construct it—but when all the benefits and costs were estimated the line was found to be socially profitable. Another example: it was found in the United States that lighthouses, whose task is to prevent shipwrecks, were far more expensive than equipping vessels with radar.

The second characteristic of public investment appraisal, which we have already indicated, is that because many relevant costs and benefits have no obvious market valuation, methods of imputing values to such items have had to be developed. We have already mentioned one example of an item with no obvious monetary valuation—time. In transport projects the major benefits are savings in time and although the value of working time is relatively obvious, most savings are of leisure time. A number of different techniques have been developed to put a value on a unit of leisure time and they come up with results which suggest that individuals value their leisure time at something like a fifth of their wage. Other examples of costs and benefits to which money values have to be imputed are mortality, noise, education and the classic case of a Norman church. There are some costs—for example the destruction of an area of natural beauty—which are normally accepted as being unquantifiable and a verbal description is all that is attempted.

The point of cost benefit analysis is to see, first, whether the expected benefits of a proposed course of action outweigh its costs, and, second, whether, in cases where there are two courses of action for roughly the same objective, one is more beneficial than the other.

Obviously, calculations of this kind raise great difficulties of an almost metaphysical nature. What is one man's cost is another man's pleasure. And what some people would call a benefit others would call a very great harm. So the more important or cosmic the question that you seek to answer, the less likely you are to find agreement. But what such a methodology can do is to define the exact area of disagreement and, sometimes, to give the disagreement a quantitative expression. For example, within the budget for arts and culture, there are items for maintaining and expanding the national collections of paintings and art objects and the annual expenditure on maintaining the public library system. There can be a clear choice (within a given total) between books and pictures, and, while there is usually a let-out—such as spending more on both books and pictures and less on something else—in fact such choices do have to be made. Perhaps numbers help, but there is a danger here. Numbers have an air of precision about them which may be, in this context, totally misleading. For they hide the large degree of artibrariness which surrounds the evaluation of costs and benefits.

It is at this stage that the idea of *output budgeting* is useful. If our objective (say, raising the cultural level of young people), can be reasonably defined, there is a variety of policies that can be adopted to achieve this end. Normally, the practice is to separate the budget for libraries, art galleries, music and school journeys. But under a system of output budgeting it would be seen that a combination of these items was in fact a means of raising the cultural level of young people. When the budget is defined in relation to a series of objectives of this kind—raising the cultural level, improving the physical standards, improving the health of young people—then the variety of paths that may be followed tend to arrange themselves into a hierarchy, or a series of hierarchies, which enable the choices to be more clearly seen. It is for this reason that in recent years the organisation of central and local government has tended to be arranged around objectives rather than functions, so that the resources may be best utilised by reference to their ultimate purpose, rather than according to the relative strength of various pressure-groups or lobbies, which has been the usual way of setting public expenditure priorities.

## Health

There are three main fields of public expenditure—health, education and defence—all very large, in which the older and newer methods of allocating resources have led to different results. In all of these the outcomes of policy are diverse and difficult to measure against particular programmes. It is therefore of great importance that the objectives should be specified as exactly as possible, and that periodic reviews should be undertaken which will enable redundant programmes to be eliminated.

Health care falls into three sectors: preventive medicine; community care, including the general practitioners and pharmacists; and hospitals. Of these by far the most costly is hospitalisation. A simple example of the relation of costs is the development of vaccines against diseases like tuberculosis. By an effective vaccination programme, the disease can be very effectively reduced, and therefore expenditure on sanatoria is virtually eliminated. Another example is lung cancer, which is almost entirely due to cigarette smoking. An effort in anti-smoking campaigns would be worth while up to the cost of the treatment of lung cancer, plus the loss of income and happiness due to the annual premature death of a substantial proportion of the older age group. Similarly, a major cause of expenditure on the hospital service is surgery after road accidents. The greater part of these accidents are due to driving at speed. The loss of working time consequent upon the enforcement of a very low speed limit could be weighed against the extremely heavy cost of road accidents.

It follows that the application of techniques of economic reasoning to patterns of health care would emphasise prevention and social medicine, rather than hospitalisation, and would tend to support investment in pharmaceuticals rather than surgery. Neither set of arguments is conclusive, but the fact that until recently they were rarely heard is an indication of the changes that may be seen in the pattern of health care as a result of the adoption of such techniques.

## Education

The results of medical care may be uncertain, but they exist. The results of education are so vague that it is almost impossible to apply any rational techniques to the subject at all, if the criterion of expenditure is to be educational outcomes. As a result educational inputs are used as surrogate for outcomes. Most industrialised countries spend over 7% of their GNP on education; the compulsory period of schooling is between 10 and 12 years, with substantial pre- and post-school provision. For each level of education there is an accepted standard of inputs; for example, that at primary school level the maximum size of class should be 35; that the curriculum in the secondary schools should include a reasonable range of subjects and activities. Thus educational expenditure is determined by the size of the school population, which is dependent on the birth-rate, plus immigration, the school leaving age and the proportion of children who stay on beyond it, and the standards of provision at various levels.

The question has been frequently raised whether there are other objective criteria which could determine the appropriate level of educational expenditure. One is the need of the economy for qualified manpower, if this need could be quantified. It is of course most extraordinarily difficult to do so, and many would argue that it is in principle impossible to do so, but if some acceptable way were found, then the necessary rate of inflow could be quantified, by relation to the desired total stock of people with appropriate qualification and the rate by which this stock is depleted by retirement and death. This flow of qualified entrants into employment should be equal to the desired outflow from education; and the shape of the education system would be determined to meet this end. It would thus be a matter of cost effectiveness to determine the least-cost course of producing, say, an aeronautics engineer.

In this connection it is important to realise that the costs are not only those borne by the public authorities, but also include the income forgone by those studying, who would otherwise probably be earning (had they been able to find a job).

An alternative criterion for allocating resources in education is what is termed the *rate-of-return approach*. This is a form of cost benefit analysis applied to education. If we take the case of University education, this can be seen as an example of public investment. The costs can be readily calculated—teachers, buildings, income forgone by students and so on—but what are the returns? The argument is that the higher a person's educational attainment, the higher his contribution to national output; it is further assumed that relative outputs are reflected in relative pay. Thus the earnings differential between a graduate and someone with an immediately lower level of academic qualification—Advanced Levels, say—is taken to be the return on investment in higher education. But it is usually accepted that only part of such earnings differentials are due to education, the rest being explained by differences in intelligence, drive and social class. Thus, estimates of the social rate of return on education have to be interpreted very cautiously and the whole approach has been subject to a fair degree of criticism.

Another criterion for expenditure on education is the so-called social demand—that which people express for their own progress, or which the authorities express to achieve greater social, sexual or racial equality. The problem here is that if a similar approach were made to other forms of public expenditure the public sector would probably claim the whole of national output.

So far none of these approaches has been successful in giving criteria that enable one course of action to be judged as more effective than another.

## Defence

That is not, however, the case with defence. In principle, expenditure on defence could be infinite—or zero. To prevent a nuclear attack from Russia or China would require a sophisticated defence system that would cost far more than the total gross national product of the United Kingdom. On the other hand, it is possible to argue that anything short of this expenditure is pointless, so it is not worth spending very much. Both postures are adopted—defence expenditures in both the USSR and USA are both greater than UK GNP; while the Irish Republic spends virtually nothing on defence. Most countries in fact fall some way between these two extremes—seeking to defend themselves by treaties (like NATO) which coalesce different countries' defence expenditure, and by defence forces which would discourage local aggression and internal subversion.

Given these objectives, in a world where military technology changes quickly, there is an infinite series of possible responses. Traditionally, a pattern of two or three hierarchical services has developed—the army, navy and the air force—which have pursued their own objectives. The story of the last fifty years of defence organisation has been some attempt to integrate these services into one strategic arm. In those countries where this has been achieved, the attempt is made strictly to define objectives, and then to delineate the means of achieving them without any regard for whichever of the services is involved. Thus, if the correct response to a military threat is an airstrike, it may not be necessary to have as many infantry regiments as the army would wish.

The efficiency of this sort of planning depends upon two considerations. The first is the extent to which the judgement as to the strategic situation is correct. Where services are integrated, an error of judgement can be overwhelming, whereas maintaining three separate services allows for alternative strategies. The second consideration is the detailed efficiency with which the services fulfil the role outlined for them. In the case of Vietnam, the first war fought with the help of neo-classical economists, the United States lost on both counts.

## The nationalised industries

In Britain, as in many of the OECD countries, several major industries are owned by the State. Most of these were taken into public ownership in 1945–51, during the term of office of the first post-war Labour government. The industries then nationalised were railways and road haulage, gas, electricity, coal, steel and also the Bank of England. It is incorrect to see this bout of nationalisation as a sudden break from free enterprise, for successive governments since 1919 had interfered in a variety of ways with the running of most of these industries.

The arguments usually advanced for nationalisation are a mixture of economic and political elements. As the economic arguments are everywhere the same but the extent of nationalisation is not, it is clear that political or philosophical considerations are dominant. We saw earlier that public ownership has long been a central tenet of socialism and allied to this is the view that the operation of basic industries like power and steel is too important to be left in private hands. In Britain, too, the post-war bout of nationalisation has to be seen in its historical context which is that by 1945 many of the industries had been starved of capital in the preceding twenty years and it seemed unlikely that the existing owners could finance the huge investment programme that was needed.

The economic arguments are usually based on the notion that some industries are subject to large economies of scale so that private enterprise would always tend to lead to monopolistic conditions. That is, these industries are what are termed 'natural monopolies'. If that is the case, the argument goes, it is best that they be state monopolies. There is also the fact that in the case of railways the cost and demand conditions are usually such that it is impossible for a railway network to run at a profit. Thus if you want a railway system it has to be partly financed by taxation. This meets with the objection that if this is the case why have a railway system at all? Railways may, however, be an activity which generates external benefits in the form of reducing congestion and pollution caused by the alternative, road transport.

Opposition to nationalisation—apart from that based upon a rejection of socialism—is normally founded upon the view that to nationalise an industry is to insulate it from the forces of the market and hence to foster inefficiency. This is a difficult hypothesis to test because continual government interference with their pricing policies has meant that the normal test of profitability is inappropriate (it would be in any case as the nationalised industries are monopolies).

The nationalised industries operate under specific statutes which lay various duties upon them, but which in each case require them to balance their books 'taking one year with another'. Subsidies are paid for specific social ends, for instance when the railways are required to run services that local communities require but which fare receipts do not cover. This leaves the industries' boards with nominal commercial independence. Two problems arise. One is the rate of return on capital they should seek. Should it be the rate on government loans, or higher, since commercial risk is involved, or lower as they are socialised? Second, should they raise money for new capital expenditure from the market, from government, or from their own resources?

If money is to be raised through the market, then they have to have real (as opposed to nominal) commercial independence and, in particular, run the risk of going bankrupt because, if the government always bails them out when the projects they invest in turn out to be uneconomic, then it is easier to raise the necessary funds through the public purse. But if that is done, then the government should have not only the right but the duty to see that public funds are not risked unnecessarily. If money for investment is raised from retained funds, then prices must be higher than they would otherwise be.

Thus the central question is how far the industries are independent, in pricing policy and in operation. Where pricing is concerned, it is always in the interests of a particular government to keep nationalised industries' prices down. But this distorts the pattern of use of resources because, if an 'economic' price were paid, the pattern of supply and demand might well be different. And, too, policies such as these severely limit the independence of nationalised industries. For instance, the closing of a steelworks is often a political act in a particular region. So, too, is a switch by a British nationalised airline from British-produced aircraft to American aircraft.

The result is that the commercial operation of the nationalised industries is severely constrained by political reality, whatever the statutes say. Some nationalised industries in Britain, particularly gas and electricity, have fairly consistently earned surpluses. As a group, however, as a result of government interference the nationalised industries are continually adding to their own and hence to the public debt, which has, at least partly, to be financed from general taxation.

## Local authorities

A parallel case arises with local authorities. The local authorities, that is county and district councils, are responsible for housing, planning, education, social and environmental services, as laid down under specific statutes. They are financed by a local property tax, the rates, and, for two-thirds of their expenditure, by special grants and a general grant from the central government, which is related to the size of their population and its 'needs', which includes an element of redistribution from richer to poorer parts of the country. On capital account they are financed by government-backed loans.

In practice their expenditure is closely regulated by central government, in the sense that the Departments of Education and Science, the Environment, and Health and Social Services are responsible for administering Acts of Parliament which enjoin local authorities to carry out specific tasks. There are areas of discretion, of course, but the differences in expenditure which result from differences between local authorities are very small indeed.

But, interestingly enough, despite the fact that Parliament has passed these Acts, and that their operation is closely supervised by departments of state, and that two-thirds of the money is found by central government, in fact the operation of local government has developed a logic of its own which defies, or appears to defy, the attempts of the Treasury to control it. Repeated attempts have been made to restrain local authority spending by Chancellors of the Exchequer; repeatedly these attempts have failed. Partly it is because the 500 or so local authorities are representative elected bodies, and so have political power of their own, but mainly it is because the government is reluctant at any point to attempt to reverse the major legislative acts under which local authorities perform their duties. It is one thing to enjoin economy, which saves pencils and paper. It is another to reduce the school leaving age which would really save money.

## Assessment

The public sector has grown dramatically in three bursts—in the First World War, in the Second World War and since the later part of the 1950s. It is like middle-aged spread. A series of good meals after marriage, and after the family is born, transforms a slender pair into substantial figures who can rarely regain their proper weight.

*Table 12*

*Total Government Expenditure as % of GNP in Selected Years*

| | | | |
|---|---|---|---|
| 1910 | 12·8 | 1935 | 24·4 |
| 1913 | 12·4 | 1939 | 34·9 |
| 1917 | 38·9 | 1940 | 59·9 |
| 1918 | 51·6 | 1944 | 72·5 |
| 1920 | 26·1 | 1950 | 39·5 |
| 1925 | 24·2 | 1955 | 37·3 |

*Source: p. 166, Peacock and Wiseman, The Growth of Public Expenditure in the United Kingdom (OUP 1961).*

The dramatic increase in Government expenditure during periods of war (expressed here as a percentage of the GNP at 1900 prices) and its considerably smaller decrease afterwards is shown in Table 12.

The growth of the public sector carries with it fantastic problems. One, which has already been discussed, is the difficulty of integrating its various aspects, and relating them to one another so that a consistent policy is followed. For example, in 1971, the Conservative government sought to make all nationalised industries profit-making concerns, but at the same time enjoined them to keep their prices down as part of the anti-inflationary policy—a problem that recurred in 1975. An attempt to restrain local authority spending involves raising council house rents, which in turn raises the outlays on social security because it raises the officially defined poverty threshold. Perhaps the major problem is that the growth of the public sector necessarily increases the gap between gross pay (the pay that a worker thinks he earns, and which his trade union negotiates) and what he takes home as net pay. Thus the effect of the growth of the public sector is in this sense disillusioning and inflationary.

Allied to this is the extremely serious problem of the fact that so large a proportion of the working population are state employees. This necessarily means that for whole segments of the working force—teachers, lawyers, doctors, miners, railway workers—there are no 'market' rates of pay. All professors, heart surgeons and railway engine drivers are state employees. On what principle is the government to settle their pay? In the case of office cleaners, the civil service has to pay the going rate, or its offices will stay dirty. But there is nowhere else for surgeons or train drivers to go, unless they emigrate.

This means that there are whole sectors of the population whose wages are settled by arbitration, by wise men, by comparability—and all these cases become political, are pressed by the unions politically on the government of the day, and their settlement affects the survival of that government. If it refuses to pay a settlement that is satisfactory to the miners, it fails, as in 1974; or it may win, as with the bus drivers in 1958. But the issue is inescapably political, as has been found time and time again, and it is infinitely easier for the government, in case after case, to settle in favour of the particular group. This creates enormous problems for the government itself, since it is faced with ever-increasing public sector settlements.

Finally, and most important of all, the existence of a large public sector carries with it an inflationary danger. The competing claims of the various departments for funds constantly tend to run ahead of current tax revenues. Increases in taxes are unpopular and so are cuts in public expenditure and the temptation simply to print money to cover the gap is often too strong. We have seen in Chapter 3 that government deficits—or increases in the money supply—have been the major cause of inflation. Of course, a large public sector does not *per se* lead to inflation because, given the will, the expenditure can always be financed by taxation; often, however, this is not the case.

### FURTHER READING

The material is well covered by A. Atkinson's *The Economics of Inequality* (Oxford, 1975), which is particularly good value for money.

# 8

# Pay and the Distribution of Income and Wealth

## Introduction

The subject matter of this chapter is of central personal concern to most of us. We shall look at the determinants of pay, and at various dimensions of the way in which the national income and wealth is distributed.

We shall start at an aggregate level with what is termed the *functional distribution of income*—the way in which income is shared between the factors that produce it. The largest share of the national income is taken by earnings, and we look at the determinants of relative earnings and the subsequent distribution of earnings. The third aspect of distribution and perhaps that which has received greatest attention is how income (that is all forms of income, not just earnings) is distributed between persons. A knowledge of the functional distribution of income and of the distribution of earnings is necessary to understand the inter-personal distribution of income. An understanding of the way in which wealth is distributed is also necessary and this is the subject of our final section.

In each case we shall describe both the existing distribution and trends over time. The whole subject of the distribution of income and wealth has aroused fierce debate and we shall look at the arguments for and against greater equality and the role that the government has played, and could play, in securing more (or less) equality. This is an area in which, for reasons that will become apparent, the 'facts' are in dispute, which makes rational discussion more difficult.

## The functional distribution of income

The distribution of the national income has long been of central importance in political economy—to explain distribution was, for example, a major aim of classical economists such as Ricardo and J. S. Mill. Changes in the distribution of factor incomes are likely to be major influences on the distribution of personal income.

In Table 13, four factor shares are distinguished—income from employment, income from self-employment, profits and rent. The share of each factor is expressed as a percentage of Gross Domestic Product.

*Table 13*

*Factor Shares in Gross Domestic Product*

| | *Income from employment* | *Income from self-employment* | *Profits* | *Rent* |
|---|---|---|---|---|
| 1922 | 62 | 16 | 14 | 7 |
| 1932 | 64 | 14 | 12 | 10 |
| 1938 | 61 | 13 | 17 | 9 |
| 1946 | 66 | 13 | 17 | 5 |
| 1952 | 66 | 11 | 19 | 4 |
| 1962 | 69 | 9 | 17 | 6 |
| 1972 | 69 | 9 | 12 | 8 |
| 1975 | 73 | 9 | 9 | 8 |

*Sources: The British Economy: Key Statistics 1900–66*
*National Income and Expenditure, 1965–75.*

*Note:* Columns do not always sum to 100 due to rounding.

---

If we look at the whole period covered by these figures we can see that the major change has been an increase in the share of income from employment at the expense of the share of the self-employed. The main cause has been a change in the number in each group—the proportion of the working population that is self-employed has halved.

Table 13 gives a slightly misleading impression of the long-run trend in profits' share. This is because profits were very depressed in the inter-war period and if we go back to the thirty years before 1919 we find that the share of profits probably averaged around 20%. If we confine our attention to the post Second World War period we see that little change occurred until the end of the 1960s (profits' share in 1968 was 16%) since when the share of profit has declined.

There is no single unambiguous way to calculate factor shares. The decline in the share of profit, for example, is more dramatic if the calculation is made on alternative bases. For example it can be argued that all of the figures should be shown net of capital consumption (depreciation). The profits shown in Table 13 are gross trading profits and it has been suggested that as part of these have to make good depreciation of the capital stock, a truer indication is given by net trading profits. Similarly the amount by which property and the assets of the self-employed have depreciated should be deducted from rent and self-employment income respectively. It is possible to allocate, in a rough and ready way, most of capital consumption between profits, rent and self-employment income. If the income going to each factor is now expressed as a percentage of Net Domestic Product (Gross Domestic Product less capital consumption), the effect is to increase the share of income from employment (which has no deduction for capital consumption) at the expense of each of the three other sources of income. The trend in distribution from the Second World War to 1967 is not significantly altered but the decline in the share of profits since 1968 is now more dramatic. The share of gross profits in the Gross Domestic Product fell from 16% to 12% between 1968 and 1973: when calculated net of capital consumption, profits' share falls from 11% to 6%.

The proportion of the Gross Domestic Product paid in the form of rent has declined slightly since 1921 although it has nearly doubled in the last twenty years. Most of this increase has been due to the growth of *imputed rent*, which now accounts for one half of all rent. This form of rent does not reflect a monetary transaction but is a flow of income assumed to accrue to those who own their own dwellings. The reason for imputing a rent to owner-occupiers is as follows: if a man purchased a house and then let it, he would receive a rent which would appear in the national accounts. If, however, he lives in the house himself there is no money flow although the same flow of services (accommodation) exists. Thus in the national accounts a rent based upon rateable values is imputed. Not everyone is happy with this method, pointing out that the valuation is fairly arbitrary and, more fundamentally, that logically one should then also impute some income to the owners of cars, television sets and so on.

In some respects a more interesting way of dividing the product is simply between those who work and those who own capital, land and property—a division that is obscured in the traditional four-fold classification of income sources. The only difficulty in calculating factor shares in this way is how to treat

*Table 14*

*Factor Shares in Gross Domestic Product*

| | *Employment Income* | *Property Income* |
|---|---|---|
| 1922 | 72 | 27 |
| 1932 | 74 | 26 |
| 1938 | 69 | 31 |
| 1946 | 75 | 25 |
| 1952 | 74 | 26 |
| 1962 | 75 | 25 |
| 1972 | 75 | 25 |
| 1975 | 79 | 21 |

*Notes and sources: See Table 13*

income from self-employment. Part of the income of a self-employed person is employment income and part will represent profit arising from the capital he employs in his business and from his risk-taking. Averaging over all self-employed persons it is probable that the best approximation is to assume that one third of self-employment income is profit, the rest being employment income. The resulting estimates are given in Table 14.

These estimates show a very slight increase in the share of employment income, broadly defined, although little change is evident since the war.

It is difficult to make precise comparisons with distribution in other countries but it is probable that the division of the product is roughly similar in industrial countries. The share of labour is probably a little higher than average in the United Kingdom and the United States, and a little lower than average in France and Belgium. It seems that during this century the share of employment income has increased in all industrial countries.

## The reasons for change in the functional distribution of income

A rough summary of changes in distribution this century would be that there has been a slight increase in the share of employment income at the expense of property income (profits and rent). The share of profits was depressed in the inter-war period and was close to its pre-1914 level in the years after the Second World War: it has fallen considerably since 1968.

A variety of theories now exists to explain changes in factor shares. Most theories seek to emphasise one particular set of forces but we are dealing with the division of a very complex aggregate and it seems unlikely that we will ever have a complete explanation. It also seems likely that the relative importance of the various influences on distribution will change over time.

We can attempt, however, a very simplified explanation which illustrates some of the major forces affecting distribution. We start with the probability that Trade Unions attempt to increase the share of income going to labour. They attempt this in the first instance by pushing for higher money wages. We saw in Chapter 3 that some economists deny that Trade Unions have any independent power to increase money wages but here we will assume that in certain circumstances Trade Unions have the independent power to gain an increase in money wages. What happens to labour's share as a result will depend upon the ability of firms to pass on the increased wage costs to consumers in the form of higher prices. If firms were able to maintain profit margins by adjusting prices to cover fully their higher wage bill then in absolute money terms wages, prices and profits would all be higher but relative shares would not be altered. (There may be some redistribution *within* each factor share but that is not our concern here.) So we have to enquire into the ability of firms (as a group) to increase prices. This ability will be greatest when aggregate demand for goods and services is relatively high, as it is in a demand inflation, and when international competition is not particularly severe. In general the circumstances, such as full employment, in which Trade Unions are likely to have the greatest bargaining power are also those in which firms find it easiest to increase prices.

The biggest shifts in factor shares have thus occurred when Unions have been successful in raising money wages yet firms have been unable fully to cover the increased wage costs. In 1921–2 Unions prevented earnings *falling* as fast as prices and profits were squeezed so that profits' share of GDP fell from 22% to 14%. In the years after 1968 profits were again squeezed as severe international competition (which was only partly ameliorated by the fall in the exchange rate) and (in some years) price control prevented firms from maintaining profit margins.

In the short term, firms can only make very small changes in their production methods. In particular the ratio in which firms employ labour and capital equipment is fairly inflexible in the short term. Over longer periods of time this is not so, however. As machines and factories wear out and come to be replaced, firms are able, within limits, to choose between various production methods which will vary in the ratios in which labour and capital are employed. An important influence on the choice of method will be, as we saw in Chapter 5, the relative prices of these inputs. If labour increases in price relative to capital equipment, then we would expect firms to choose techniques which are relatively more capital-intensive. This is in fact what has happened. This century the price of labour has increased relative to the price of capital and the amount of capital used has increased by at least two or three times as much as employment. The impact of such changes on distribution will depend upon how easy it is for firms to substitute capital for labour. Thus if the price of labour rises 5% relative to the price of capital then labour's share of the national income will rise, fall or stay the same according to whether employment falls relative to the amount of capital employed by less, more or equal to 5% respectively.

It is also possible that an increase in the cost of labour-intensive methods relative to that of capital-intensive methods may stimulate innovations which employ less labour. The evidence on this is far from clear but in general we can say that the nature of technological change, in the sense of whether it leads to the use of more or less labour-intensive techniques, will influence distribution.

We have thus identified four influences upon how the national income is distributed but it is not in general possible to say anything about the relative importance of each. This is a pity because the implications of the various possibilities are considerable. Say, for example, Trade Unions have little power to increase labour's share, which is a view held by some economists. This would mean that the role of Trade Unions would then be to determine the distribution of labour's share, rather than the distribution of the national income.

## The determinants of relative pay

Here we are interested in what determines the pay of an individual relative to others. Everything we know about the wage determination process tells us that it is relative pay that is held to be important and this is very reasonable as it is only in relationship to others that a person can judge whether his pay is high or low. The earnings determination process is very complex and there does not exist a simple explanation of pay differentials that can cope with the variety of experience in the real world. What we can do is to sketch out the main influences on relative pay indicating those that *in general* are likely to be the most important.

The main influence on the pay of most workers will be their skill and educational attainments. There are some economists who believe that this can be seen as a complete explanation with other factors simply providing some random variance of earnings levels around those predicted by skill. The *human capital* explanation of differentials is as follows: assume that at the end of compulsory schooling everyone has the same earnings capacity. Some enter the labour market straight away, going into unskilled manual jobs. Others stay on at school or in some other way (on-the-job training for example) acquire more skills and qualifications. These latter groups will be incurring costs, largely in the form of the income they forgo through not working. The return on this investment comes in the form of lifetime earnings higher than those received by the unskilled. If the return on acquiring any given skill or qualification, expressed as a *rate* of return on the investment in skill acquisition, is low relative to some normal or expected return, then the numbers entering it will decline and vice versa. On this view the higher earnings of the skilled are just enough to compensate them for the costs of their education and training.

One has to make many assumptions to generate this explanation but the crucial one is that outlined above. However, IQ and socio-economic background exert an independent influence on earnings and hence the assumption that all have equal earnings capacity at the end of compulsory schooling does not hold. But there seems little doubt that for most workers their occupation, defined in terms of their training and education, is the main influence upon their earnings.

At the upper end of the earnings scale this ceases to be a satisfactory explanation of pay. The special responsibilities of managers require different skills to those attained from formal training but they are rewarded in the same ways. Some high earners, such as entertainers, possess non-reproducible skills; their earnings are often referred to as 'rents of ability'.

The industry a person works in exerts an influence on his earnings. That is, someone with similar skills will tend to earn different amounts in different industries. An example of this is the car industry where job-for-job earnings are higher than in the rest of the engineering industry. The reasons for the existence of industrial earnings differentials is not fully understood. Earnings do tend to be higher in industries with a high degree of industrial concentration (see Chapter 6) where plant size also tends to be large.

As if this were not enough there is considerable evidence that people with the same skill and working in the same industry will have different earnings according to which firm they work for. Studies show that in a given area earnings for similar workers in highest-paying firms are often as much as twice those in the lowest-paying firm in the industry. Although we would not expect there to be no such differences in earnings, the size of these differentials is rather surprising. One explanation is that employers make a conscious decision to be a low payer or a high payer. High payers will be able to impose stricter recruiting standards and will experience lower rates of labour turnover. Thus differences in pay will not reflect differences in total labour costs (wages plus recruitment and training costs) per unit of output.

Among other determinants of pay that we should mention are the relative strengths of different unions and professional associations, sex, race and region. It is difficult to assess the impact that unions can have on pay as in Britain, unlike the United States, one cannot compare a non-unionised and a unionised sector of an industry and, further, many unions are organised in a way that cuts across industry divisions. The United States' evidence suggests that earnings in unionised sectors are about 5–7% above those in non-unionised parts of industry. This suggests that it is easy to over-estimate union power. It is likely that powerful unions emerge in areas where conditions arc anyway favourable to high earnings. However, this is not to deny that in a few industries and occupations employee organisations do have the ability to raise relative earnings significantly, usually by controlling entry into the occupation. The printing unions and the Bar association are good examples.

Women usually earn less than men and this is paradoxically true even in occupations like teaching where equal pay has been the rule for a long time. Ethnic minorities also experience relatively low earnings. It is probable that a large part of such earnings differences are explicable in terms of education and training although some overt discrimination exists. Regional differences in earnings are very small in Britain.

Finally over and above all this is the importance of what Lydall has termed the D-factor—standing for determination, drive, dynamism and doggedness. By this is meant that even if we could standardise for education, occupation, industry, sex, race and so on, we would still observe earnings differences due to these personal characteristics.

We can measure differences in people's pay on the basis of a number of alternative groupings. We can, for example, take differences in the pay of people working in different industries or in different occupations, firms, regions and so on. If we do this we find that, whatever basis we use, pay differentials change very little over time. This is seen most dramatically in the case of the inter-personal distribution of earnings—and we consider this in detail in the next section.

The force of custom is probably the main reason for stability of pay differentials. People can only judge whether their pay is fair by making comparisons with the pay of others, and once a set of wage relativities evolves historically people will see it as 'fair' if they maintain their place in the pay rankings. However, over periods of time some groups may slowly slip back on the pay scale, and there comes a time when they perceive this as unfair and take action to remedy it. An example, in Britain, would be miners who fell from near the top of the industrial pay rankings around 1960 to the middle at the end of the decade. Mounting resentment at this state of affairs led to industrial action culminating in the Wilberforce enquiry which recognised the strength of claims based on this decline.

So movement does take place but is often reversed. The stability of pay differentials has an important implication for the framing of incomes policies that we discussed in Chapter 4. Stability of differentials implies, of course, that earnings increase each year by very similar amounts in different industries and occupations, and thus movements of labour seem to occur without any change in relative wages. There is, therefore, no need in an incomes policy to allow exceptions on the grounds of a shortage of labour in a particular industry or occupation. To do so would in fact threaten the effectiveness of an incomes policy for it would set up demands—on the grounds of fairness

—for the exceptional increase to be copied elsewhere. Incomes policies do have to be sufficiently flexible, however, to cater for groups who feel that the wage structure at the start of the policy was not fair, for example because they were about to reach a settlement when the policy was imposed.

## The distribution of earnings

We have seen that a person's relative pay is the outcome of a wide variety of influences. We now need some way of measuring how equally or unequally earnings are distributed. We are talking of distribution between 25 million people and to get very far we need some method of summarising the distribution. We need therefore to explain one or two simple statistical terms that we shall use both here and in the subsequent section.

All readers will be familiar with the concept of average (or mean) earnings—the total amount of earnings divided by the number of earners. We will use another sort of average called the *median*. The median is the income figure which divides the number of earnings into two equal parts. Thus half the earnings are below and half the earnings are above the median value. So if we enquired into the median earnings of 21 workers then, if we ranked them according to their earnings, the median would be the earnings of the eleventh man—ten men would earn more and ten men less than the eleventh man.

We can similarly define the *lowest decile:* this is the wage level below which 10% of the number of earnings fall, 90% of workers earning more than this. We can also record the values of the *lower quartile*, *upper quartile* and *upper decile:* these are respectively the wage levels below which 25%, 75% and 90% of earners fall.

A convenient way of summarising a distribution is to express these four quartiles as a percentage of the median. This is done in Table 15.

The earnings of non-manual workers are more widely dispersed than those of manual workers. This is what we would expect from our discussion of occupational pay differentials, where we concluded that many pay differences exist to compensate for differential training costs. There will be greater differences in training and education between non-manual workers than between manual workers.

*Table 15*

*Distribution of Gross Weekly Earnings, 1975 (quartiles as a percentage of the median)*

| | *Lower decile* | *Lower quartile* | *Upper quartile* | *Upper decile* |
|---|---|---|---|---|
| Manual men | 69·2 | 82·8 | 121·3 | 144·4 |
| Non-manual men | 6·26 | 77·5 | 129·6 | 166·7 |
| Manual women | 68·4 | 83·3 | 119·6 | 141·4 |
| Non-manual women | 66·5 | 80·3 | 127·2 | 171·5 |

*Source: Department of Employment Gazette 1975*

Now we move on to look at changes over time in the dispersion of earnings. Here we find a very striking fact. The dispersion of earnings has remained virtually unchanged for nearly a century.

*Table 16*

*Distribution of Weekly Earnings of Male Manual Workers (quartiles expressed as % of median)*

| | *Lowest decile* | *Lowest quartile* | *Highest quartile* | *Highest decile* |
|---|---|---|---|---|
| 1886 | 68·6 | 82·8 | 121·7 | 143·1 |
| 1938 | 67·6 | 82·1 | 118·5 | 139·9 |
| 1960 | 70·6 | 82·6 | 120·7 | 143·0 |
| 1975 | 69·2 | 82·8 | 121·3 | 144·4 |

*Source: Department of Employment Gazette 1974*

This is seen most clearly in the case of manual workers, for whom we have the most complete statistics. In Table 16 we show the distribution of earnings of male manual workers for various years since 1886.

In 1886 median weekly earnings were £1·21; in 1975 they

were £53·2. Thus over a period of 90 years during which money earnings increased over forty-fold the dispersion of earnings has changed very little.

This conclusion has to be modified only slightly if we include non-manual workers so as to look at the distribution of the earnings of all employees. In this case the dispersion has narrowed slightly at the upper end—say above the highest decile. The cause of this has been the decline in the relative position of professional groups which has been the main change this century in occupational pay differentials. This has largely resulted from the great expansion of education which has increased the supply of entrants to these groups. At the same time social class barriers have been eroded, making entry into professional occupations considerably easier.

The overall picture is one of stability. It is not clear exactly why there is this seemingly immutable law that says, for example, that the lowest decile of manual workers should get about 69% of median earnings. It seems likely that the main thing holding the structure together is the widespread use of comparability in wage negotiations. This is accepted by both sides to a wage bargain as being a fair and reasonable agreement. It does not seem likely, however, that this on its own could produce the almost complete stability that we observe.

## The distribution of personal income

We are now in a position to discuss the distribution of personal incomes. By this term we mean incomes that accrue to persons. The major sources of personal income are income from employment (earnings) and self-employment, investment income, rent and various payments such as pensions, made by public authorities.

There are various sources of information on the distribution of personal incomes, none of which are perfectly satisfactory. The figures we use here are derived from the estimates produced in the National Accounts and are largely based upon tax returns made to the Inland Revenue. These are generally thought to be the most reliable figures although they do possess many shortcomings. It would be tedious to detail all of these but it is important to point out some of the more serious weaknesses of the published statistics.

The units used in the tables are neither individuals nor households but some combination of the two. This is because the incomes of married women are aggregated, for tax purposes, with the incomes of their husbands. As the material comes originally from tax returns only that income which is liable to tax is included. Over the years a large number of tax avoidance methods—many of which convert income into capital—have been developed and hence a person's income for tax purposes may not correspond to his real income (his command over resources). No interest which is tax-deductible appears in the figures. Thus a man with an income of £10 000 a year with a mortgage and a bank loan on which the interest amounts to £3000 will appear in the table as having an income of £7000. Finally the way in which non-taxable benefits (e.g. pensions) are added into the distribution is open to some error. Thus the figures are least reliable at the bottom of the distribution.

Table 17 shows the share of total personal income going to each income range group.

In 1972 (the latest year for which we have data) the top 10% of income recipients received 26·9% of personal income while the bottom half of income recipients received only 24% of personal income. It may help to put these figures in perspective if we give a few examples of the absolute figures. In 1972 to be in the top 1% you would need an income of at least £6236, to be in the top 10% an income of £2857. The median was £1338.

The table also shows post-war trends in the distribution of income. The main change has been the decline in the share of the top 5% of the distribution from 23·8% to 17·2%. The corresponding gains have been received not by the bottom half of the distribution but by the rest of the top half.

A truer picture of the distribution of goods and services is gained if we take account of taxation. Taxes on income are *progressive* in the sense that the higher the income of a tax unit the greater the proportion of income that is taken in tax. On the other hand indirect taxes (taxes on expenditure) are largely *regressive*—the lower one's income, the greater the proportion that is paid in the form of indirect taxes.

The net result of the progressive nature of direct taxation and the regressive nature of most indirect taxation is that the tax system taken as a whole has no effect at all on distribution. This rather surprising result has been established both for the United Kingdom and for the United States.

*Table 17*

*Distribution of Pre-Tax Incomes*

| *Income Group* | *1949* % | *1959* % | *1972* % |
|---|---|---|---|
| Top 1% | 11·2 | 8·4 | 6·4 |
| 2–5% | 12·6 | 11·5 | 10·8 |
| 6–10% | 9·4 | 9·5 | 9·7 |
| 11–20% | 14·1 | 15·1 | 15·8 |
| 21–30% | 11·2 | 12·6 | 13·1 |
| 31–40% | 9·6 | 10·7 | 11·0 |
| 41–50% | 8·2 | 9·1 | 9·2 |
| 51–60% | } | 7·5 | 7·5 |
| 61–70% | } | 5·9 | 5·9 |
| 71–80% | } 23·7 | 4·4 | 4·8 |
| 81–90% | } | } 5·3 | } 5·8 |
| 91–100% | } | } | } |

*Source: First Report of the Royal Commission on the Distribution of Income and Wealth, 1975.*

---

How is it then that the state redistributes income if the tax system is broadly neutral? The redistribution comes about through government expenditure. This is seen most obviously in the case of transfer payments such as pensions and supplementary benefits. The recipients of these benefits tend to be in the lower parts of the income distribution. Apart from redistributing income from the relatively well-off to the poor the system also favours large families relative to small families. The Central Statistical Office publishes annual estimates of the extent of redistribution when all taxes and transfer payments and government expenditure on health and education are taken into account. These estimates show that a considerable amount of redistribution occurs and, as we have seen, this is solely due to the way in which government expenditure is distributed between families with different incomes. These studies also show that there has been no noticeable change in the extent of redistribution since 1961.

## The distribution of wealth

We start by explaining what we mean by a person's (or a household's) wealth. Most people would agree that we should count as wealth bank deposits, cash in hand, shares, government securities, other loans made such as building society deposits and houses, while deducting any outstanding liabilities. Thus, for example, a person with a house worth £15 000 on which there is a mortgage of £5000 would count this as a wealth of £10 000. There are one or two items where there is some doubt, however. The first of these are claims to a future flow of income to a future capital payment. The most obvious of these claims are occupational pension schemes. Although it seems that these must be a form of wealth as they will generate an income flow in the future in the same way as a share does, there are some difficulties of valuation because pension rights are not marketable. The same comments apply to state pension rights. Whether those items are counted as wealth depends in the end upon the source of the wealth estimates, for as we shall see, there are severe problems in estimating personal wealth. Another set of items which may or may not be classed as wealth is personal effects. Where these take the form of fine antiques or valuable paintings there seems little disagreement, but what about the furniture, household goods and clothes that we possess? The normal solution to the problem is to include only consumer durable goods as it is only for these that we can get remotely accurate estimates of value.

There is no annual survey of wealth in the United Kingdom and so personal wealth has to be estimated. These estimates are usually based on Estate Duty statistics on the wealth of those who have died in any year. Using mortality tables, these are 'blown up' to derive an estimate of the wealth of the living. It is generally accepted that, for a variety of reasons, these estimates are subject to considerable error.

The figures show that wealth is highly concentrated into a few hands. If we exclude state pension rights, the top 1% of wealth holders possess nearly 28% of the personal wealth of the adult population while the top 5% as a group possess over half, which leaves less than half of personal wealth for the remaining 95%. There are almost certainly great disparities in the wealth of even the top 1%. To be included in the top 1% one would need in 1972 a wealth of at least £44 000 but also in that group

*Table 18*

*Shares in Income and Wealth, 1972 (%)*

| | *Income* | *Wealth* |
|---|---|---|
| Top 1% | 6·4 | 27·6 |
| Top 5% | 17·2 | 51·3 |
| Top 10% | 26·9 | 67·2 |
| Top 20% | 42·7 | 86·4 |

*Source: First Report of the Royal Commission on the Distribution of Income and Wealth, 1975*

we have Lord Cowdray with a reported wealth in excess of £100 million. Thus wealth is distributed in a far more unequal way than is income, as is clear from the figures in Table 18.

The form in which wealth is held varies with the amount of wealth. For example, those with between £10 000 and £20 000 held 55% of their wealth in the form of dwellings, 17% in the form of life insurance policies, and 5% in shares and securities. The super-rich, those with over £200 000, had 8% of their wealth in dwellings, 2% in life policies and 57% in shares and securities.

It seems from studies of distribution in other countries that wealth is distributed more unequally in the United Kingdom than in any other industrial country. This is not true of earnings, nor is it true of income because in these cases the United Kingdom seems to have an average, or perhaps even less than average, degree of inequality.

The distribution of personal wealth has grown markedly less unequal this century. In 1911 the share of the top 1% was about 69% (28% now) and that of the top 10% was about 92% (67% now). However, the distribution remains very unequal as the figures in Table 18 show, and it is probable that most of the redistribution has occurred in the top quarter of the distribution.

In any society where people save either to provide for themselves in old age or to pass on some capital to their sons and daughters some inequality of wealth will be inevitable and, most would argue, desirable. The great disparities in wealth that we observe do not occur in this way, as given the high rates of taxation of high incomes only a very few can accumulate fortunes out of earned incomes. The major cause of the extreme inequality is, of course, inherited wealth and many of the truly rich owe their fortunes to the acts of their ancestors. Despite high nominal rates the Estate Duty in the United Kingdom did relatively little to break up large wealth holdings as it was an easily avoidable tax paid by the unfortunate and the philanthropic.

## The debate on equality

So far we have presented some facts on distribution and have not been concerned with whether the distribution *ought* to be different. It is to this latter question that we now turn.

It has to be emphasised at the outset that there can be no objective answer to such questions as, should attempts be made to reduce the unequal distribution of income or wealth? In order to come up with policy recommendations in this area—as in others—one has to make value judgements. Even if one makes the value judgement that, for example, income should be more equally distributed, one still has to express preferences for which aspect of the distribution should be changed. Should the main concern be to reduce the share of the top 5%, or the top 10%, or should the object be to increase the share of the bottom 10%, or what?

All we can do here is to set out the arguments that have been expressed both for and against more equality and discuss the means by which distribution could be changed, should a change be desired.

Let us begin by reminding ourselves of how the existing distribution of income is generated. The largest part of personal income is made up of earnings. We saw earlier that a person's earnings are influenced by a very large number of things. To start with, we have genetic influences on his IQ which are compounded by the amount of education he receives which, in turn—at least in the United Kingdom—is heavily influenced by the socio-economic class of his parents. It is thus likely that a large part of occupational earnings differentials is explicable in terms of education. But this is far from the whole story. A person's earnings will also partly depend upon whether he is a member of a powerful Trade Union or professional association and upon which industry he works in. We saw, too, that there are large variations in earnings between different firms in the same industry. We must not forget, either, that, especially for non-manual workers, earnings vary with age. Finally we should mention what has been termed the D-factor—doggedness, determination, drive and dynamism—which seems to exert influence over and above the list of factors already given. Despite this multitude of influences we saw that the distribution of earnings has changed very little during the last 100 years.

The distribution of all personal incomes is less equal than the distribution of earnings due to the relatively unequal dispersion of income from wealth. Hence the distribution of wealth is an important determinant of income distribution. Finally changes in the functional distribution of income will lead to changes in the distribution of personal incomes.

Let us begin by looking at the arguments which have been expressed in favour of securing a more equal distribution of income. For the moment we will assume that we are talking of incomes after direct taxation and after allowance is made for transfer payments.

The case for greater equality essentially rests upon the notions of morality and fairness. It is seen as morally wrong that the rich can spend freely on luxury goods and services while the poor find it difficult to purchase basic necessities such as food, housing and clothing. It is wrong because it is largely a matter of chance whether one is rich or poor. Those with very high incomes often derive them from inherited wealth, the provision of which is an accident of birth. It is also, of course, an accident of birth whether one's genetic inheritance favours the acquisition of a high income through high earnings. There is a difference, however, between these two cases. Where a person is endowed with, say, a high IQ, or is very determined, or has whatever it is that one needs to earn a high income, he has to exert effort, say by undertaking a lengthy education, in order to generate high earnings. The person with inherited wealth has to do nothing.

We can also bring a little economics into the argument. For a long time in economics it has been suggested that income is subject to the *law of diminishing marginal utility*. This means that if we give an extra £10 to a man whose income is £20 000 the enjoyment (utility) he would get from spending it is less than the extra utility that would be gained from an extra £10 by a person whose income is £1000. Thus if we took £10 from the former and gave it to the latter their joint utility would increase. On this argument the optimal distribution of any income would be one where everyone had an identical income. For as long as some received more than others, transfers could take place which would increase the utility enjoyed by the group of income recipients. Nobody pretends, of course, that utility can be measured. All that is necessary for this argument is an acceptance of the notion that the higher one's income is the less one values any increment. Many would not accept this, arguing that one's capacity to enjoy income increases with income. Others would say that the theory is probably true if we compare people at the extremes of the income distribution, but that it is not true for, say, the middle 75% of the income distribution.

Finally, and perhaps most important, there is the argument that income should be redistributed in order to alleviate poverty. To many the alleviation of poverty is what redistribution is all about. This raises again the important issue of defining exactly what we mean by 'more equality'. As we are talking of twenty million or so income units, this is no easy task. It is hardly likely that any policy could lead to everyone below the median moving upwards and everyone above the median moving down or indeed that that is what anyone would wish. Hence to say that equality should decrease, or increase, one has to specify with which part of the distribution one is concerned. To some it is the disproportionate share of income (and wealth) taken by the top 10% that is most objectionable. Thus to them any reduction in this share would be a move towards equality, whatever happened in the rest of the distribution. For others the main concern is with the levels of income received by those at the bottom of the distribution—the poor. There are many other criteria—including purely statistical ones—which could be used. Thus there are many views on what increased equality means and there is rarely an unambiguous answer to the question of whether equality has increased or decreased. Between 1959 and 1964, for example, the share in personal income of both the top decile and the bottom two deciles declined. So, according to the criteria used, equality could be said to have increased or decreased.

That, then, is a very brief sketch of the sorts of arguments that are put forward by those who feel that the distribution of income (and *a fortiori* wealth) is inequitable in the United Kingdom. There are many who disagree. There is little disagreement about the desirability of bringing the poor to some minimum standard of living although there is dispute over the methods to be used. The basic case against more equality (or perhaps in favour of more inequality) is that differences in income are necessary to provide incentives to work, to invest and to take risks. This is clearly a strong case, as egalitarians do not argue for complete equality—everyone having the same income—which is where, for example, the principle of diminishing marginal utility of income leads. Thus the argument is about the *degree* of inequality and, as we have seen, things are not simplified by the errors in the published statistics. A second line of reasoning is that inequality is desirable because the rich have a higher propensity to save than do the poor and hence with unequal distributions, more savings are generated to finance investment. It is not likely that this argument has much force in an industrial economy and to the extent that it does, any adverse effect on investment could be offset by action to mobilise the savings of the not-so-rich.

For what it is worth, our personal view is that it is an attack on extreme inequalities in wealth holdings that is needed rather than direct action on incomes. Much income inequality is due both directly and indirectly to wealth inequality and a redistribution of wealth would also reduce income inequality.

Legislation is already either on the statute books or will shortly be introduced to reduce extreme inequalities in wealth holdings. This legislation takes the form of the Capital Transfer Tax and the introduction of a wealth tax, similar in design to those operating in many Western European countries.

In the short run, poverty can only really be alleviated by transfers. Transfers will also have to be part of the long-run story as many causes of poverty—old age, death of head of household, sickness—are simply part of life. There are some symptoms, however, that can be directly attacked. Many low paid workers also suffer from insecurity of employment. Both the low pay and the insecurity are basically due to such workers being unskilled. Therefore any long-term policy to improve the relative position of families at the bottom of the distribution should include measures to improve the education and, probably more important, the training of disadvantaged workers. At the moment there is a cycle of deprivation. Children of the poor go to poor schools, often in the declining centres of cities, to leave school early and to go into dead-end jobs. When they marry the cycle often continues. This has long been recognised and it has to be admitted that progress is very slow, even in the richest countries of the world.

FURTHER READING

A. Culver's *Social Policy* (Martin Robertson, 1973) is a good introduction to this aspect of public policy.

# 9

# International Trade and Payments

## Introduction

The economic linkages that exist between countries take many forms. The most obvious is trade in goods and in services. The size of the trade sector—as measured by the average of imports plus exports as a percentage of national income—varies considerably. An economy like that of Sweden or the United Kingdom which has a large trade sector of up to 30% of national income is referred to as a relatively 'open' one. Large countries like the United States encompassing a wide variety of climatic regions and with a diverse industrial structure tend, for reasons that will become obvious in the next section, to be relatively closed: in the United States the trade sector is about 5% of national income. Many less-developed countries have small trade sectors and this tendency may be reinforced by ideological considerations, as in the case of Albania. The next sections discuss the reasons for trade, offer an explanation of the sorts of goods and services which various countries import and export, and discuss various barriers to trade which nations impose.

These flows of goods and services give rise to flows of money in the opposite direction. Money also flows between countries for other reasons. Governments lend money to other governments, firms invest in other countries, individuals own shares in foreign companies and so on. These foreign payments are summed up in a country's Balance of Payments accounts, which are discussed in a later section.

There is no reason for the foreign payments of a nation to just equal its foreign receipts and as it is difficult for a country persistently to spend more abroad than it earns, it follows that some mechanism must exist to bring about adjustment to long-run disequilibrium in foreign payments. Subsequent sections will look at various adjustment mechanisms, and will also discuss international monetary institutions.

## The causes of trade

The traditional explanation of trade is that it is merely an international extension of the principle of specialisation which underlies much economic activity.

Take the following example which, although very simple, shows the principle clearly. Say there were just two countries, call them Southland and Northland, and each country produced just two goods, beef and steel, using only one input, labour. For the moment, assume that both goods in both countries are produced under conditions of constant marginal returns; that is, as more beef (or steel) is produced, the labour input required to produce each unit does not vary. Further, assume that there are no costs of transport between Southland and Northland. To forestall the reader's impatience with these assumptions let us say now that we will indicate later the effect of introducing more realistic conditions.

To begin with, the countries do not trade. The situation is:

*Before trade*

*Southland:* one man year of labour produces 10 units of beef, or 5 units of steel.
*Northland:* one man year of labour produces 1 unit of beef or 1 unit of steel.

We can see immediately that Southland is better at producing both goods, in the sense that a man year of labour there produces more steel or beef than a man year of labour produces in Northland. Southland, we can say, has an absolute advantage in the production of both commodities. Northland has, correspondingly, an absolute disadvantage in the production of both goods. It has, however—and this is the important point—a *comparative advantage* in the production of steel. For while a man year of labour in Southland can produce ten times as much beef as a man year of labour in Northland, it can only produce five times as much steel. As long as a comparative advantage exists, or to put it another way, as long as there is a difference in comparative costs, then through specialisation and trade the two countries will mutually gain. This can be demonstrated as follows.

In Southland the *opportunity cost* of a unit of beef is $\frac{1}{2}$ unit of steel. (By opportunity cost we mean the cost in terms of the forgone output of other commodities.) If through trade Southland can obtain more than $\frac{1}{2}$ unit of steel for one unit of beef then the country will gain. Similarly it can be seen that if Northland can, through trade, get more than one unit of beef for one unit of steel then it will also gain. Thus for trade to be profitable to both then the terms on which the goods are traded must lie between the two internal cost ratios (in this case between 1:$\frac{1}{2}$ and 1:1, the ratio of beef:steel). If the terms of trade settled at one unit of beef: $\frac{3}{4}$ unit of steel then the situation would be as follows:

*After trade*

*Southland:* two man years of labour produce 20 units of beef. 10 units retained. 10 units of beef traded for 7$\frac{1}{2}$ units of steel.

*Gain:* 2$\frac{1}{2}$ units of steel per two man years of labour.

*Northland:* two man years of labour produce 2 units of steel. One unit retained. One unit of steel traded for 1$\frac{1}{3}$ units of beef.

*Gain:* $\frac{1}{3}$ unit of beef per two man years of labour.

Through specialising in the good in which it has a comparative advantage, each country gains through trade. This is the basis of trade and it illustrates a very important point, which is that countries whose absolute costs of production are higher than another's can still profitably trade as long as there exist differences in comparative costs. This may seem odd, but put it in another context: a man may be an international pilot and a first-rate car mechanic; it still pays him to specialise in flying planes and get someone else to service his car, because his comparative advantage is greatest in flying.

This explanation of trade between two countries can now be generalised. Each country can, with respect to trade, view the rest of the world as a single unit and hence our explanation in terms of two countries remains valid. The explanation also remains valid when we allow for the multitude of goods and services that are, or could be, traded. The easiest way to cope with this is to imagine a country ranking goods in order of comparative cost: it will then tend to specialise and export these where comparative costs are lowest and import those in which it is at a comparative disadvantage. It is not quite as simple as this because an industrial country will often both import and export the same good. Cars are an obvious example of goods which can be both imported and exported. Cars are not homogeneous; there are lots of makes and models and the preferences of different consumers lead to imports and exports. In many cases, too, there will be situations where a country is a net importer of a certain type of good but some domestic producers will be able to concentrate on a specialist part of the market and export successfully. Many goods bear import tariffs and, while deferring detailed discussion of protection, it is clear that this will also explain the co-existence of imports and exports of the same type of good.

The principle shown by our simple example, that differences in comparative costs of production give rise to trade, thus underlies all international trade. Which gives rise to the question—what causes international differences in comparative costs of production? In the case of raw materials, climatic and geological conditions supply the answer. Most tropical foodstuffs could be grown in Europe under artificial conditions, for example, but the costs of production under these conditions place European producers at a disadvantage—absolutely, as well as comparatively. For manufactured goods it is differences in what are termed 'factor endowments' that provide the explanation.

If we ignore land, as being unimportant in the production of manufactured goods, we are left with labour and capital. Although it is very difficult—some would say impossible—to measure the capital stock of a country, it is clear beyond doubt that there are very marked international differences in capital to labour endowments. The ratio of the capital stock of the United States to its labour force is many times greater than that of, say, India. This gives the United States a comparative advantage in the production of goods requiring capital-intensive techniques of production, while India has a comparative advantage in labour-intensive goods. Similarly, if we break labour down into different types of labour, each defined by its skill, we could expect nations which have highly developed education and training systems to have comparative advantages in the production of goods requiring skilled labour.

These things change over time. A good example is the United Kingdom cotton textile industry. Britain was the first country to industrialise and cotton textiles was one of the goods in which the country specialised. As industrialisation spread to eastern countries it became apparent that Britain did not have a comparative advantage in the production of unsophisticated textiles which could be produced with unskilled labour and simple machinery. Countries like India and Japan possessed these endowments and in the inter-war period, employment in cotton in Britain declined from 600 000 to 200 000. The cotton industry in Britain was forced to specialise in the production of high-quality textiles requiring skilled labour and relatively more capital, in which Britain still possessed a comparative advantage. Since the war, as more advanced techniques have been introduced in various Asian countries, the British cotton industry has again been forced to concentrate increasingly on the production of higher quality goods. If one buys a cheap shirt the odds are that it will have been produced abroad, if one buys an expensive fashion shirt it will probably be British-made. Thus comparative costs of production change as factor endowments, skills and techniques of production change.

## Protection

We have seen that a country will gain through international trade in the sense of its population having more goods and services—a higher standard of living—than would be possible in the absence of trade. Despite this, virtually every country in the world imposes restrictions of various sorts upon the flow of goods and services. These restrictions have, to some extent, historical causes which we will comment on, but we begin by seeing why in principle such restrictions—which we can collectively term *protection*—are imposed.

If we could imagine an industrial country suddenly moving from being a closed economy to one that trades—as Spain did in the late 1950s—we would find it would gain. The gains would not be evenly distributed and some of the population could lose. Consumers in general would gain, as they would have more choice and would be able to buy many products at lower prices as some domestic production was replaced by imports. Those working in and owning industries which had low comparative costs would also gain as production in these industries expanded. There would be other industries which would decline. In a perfect world their resources would switch into the growing industries but in practice there will be many obstacles to such a transfer of resources. The major difficulty is that labour tends to be immobile and there is no reason to assume that the expanding industries are located in the same regions as the declining, nor that the skills possessed by the men made unemployed are those required elsewhere.

It is easy to state that a forceful regional policy and retraining programmes can overcome these obstacles, but often the severe practical difficulties and social problems that ensue are avoided by protecting the industry. The losses to certain parts of the community are reduced at the expense of reducing the gain to the whole community.

Protection can take various forms. One common method is the *tariff*, which is a tax on imports. The effect is to raise the domestic price of imports thus protecting high-cost domestic producers. Physical limitations—quotas—can be imposed. A country which has a system of exchange control can use this to provide specific protection. If people have to apply to the Central Bank in order to acquire foreign exchange to purchase imports, the Bank can refuse applications for currency which will be used to purchase certain types of goods from abroad.

Protection can take more subtle forms. A country which has health or other regulations on the content of foodstuffs, or the noise level of cars, which are markedly different from the rest of the world, is operating a form of protection. To meet these requirements foreign producers incur costs which are likely to be greater per unit than those incurred by domestic producers, as the specification of the articles has to be changed on only a part of their production. It is to eliminate these disguised impediments to trade that the European Economic Community (EEC) is attempting to standardise such regulations—although this again incurs a real cost (bureaucracy) and, perhaps, a psychic cost to consumers (uniformity).

The tariffs levied today by industrial countries are largely explicable in terms of experience in the 1930s. Although by 1919 there had been some retreat from the high days of free trade reached at the turn of the century, protection was then the exception rather than the rule. In the inter-war period and particularly during the 1930s most countries experienced high rates of unemployment and low levels of economic activity. One, almost universal, reaction was the pursuit of 'beggar-my-neighbour' policies—each country attempting to reduce domestic unemployment by cutting imports. Collectively this was, of course, a futile policy but the political pressures on governments to follow such a path were very strong. The situation in 1945 was, then, that most nations imposed tariffs on a wide range of imported goods. Individual nations are unlikely to make unilateral tariff reductions and post-war developments have taken the form of bilateral and multilateral reductions. Two sets of institutions should be mentioned in this context.

First, the General Agreement on Tariffs and Trade (GATT). This is an organisation set up in 1947 by twenty-three nations. The most important negotiations under the aegis of GATT took place in the 1960s. These mainly concerned the United States and other major industrial countries and took the form of negotiations between major suppliers and importers. Through the 'most favoured nation' clause any tariff reductions were automatically extended to all signatories of GATT.

The second set of institutions to have developed are free trade areas such as the EEC and the Latin American Free Trade Area, and the European Free Trade Area. These agreements can take the form of a progressive move towards the removal of all tariffs between the members of a free trade area or, as in the case of EEC, towards a more complete form of economic integration based upon free trade. It is fairly common in such agreements to find special exceptions granted to particular countries or industries so that some protection remains.

## The balance of payments

The financial transactions of one nation with the rest of the world are summed up in its *Balance of Payments*. Many of these transactions reflect trade in goods and services but there are other monetary flows which occur independently of trade.

The Balance of Payments accounts are, like all accounts, based upon a double-entry method and therefore must of necessity always balance. To interpret them we therefore have to sectionalise them in some way, as in Table 19. To give some idea of magnitudes we present a simplified version of the United Kingdom Balance of Payments for 1974.

The accounts have been divided into five sections. The first shows the value of trade in goods. Nearly a quarter of the import bill was accounted for by oil. Payments for oil in 1974 were over three times their level in 1973 and over four times their level in 1974. The country's trade in goods showed an overall deficit of £5259m. It is normal for the trade balance of the United Kingdom to be negative although the deficit has been vastly increased in the last two years by the increase in the price of oil.

The visible deficit was partially offset by a surplus on what is called invisible trade. One component of invisible trade is trade in services such as insurance, financial services and tourism. Insurance sold by a UK company to an overseas resident counts as an invisible export, for example, while money spent by British tourists abroad counts as an invisible import. Other forms of invisible trade are interest, profits and dividends. On balance the United Kingdom receives more in this form than it pays out. Only the annual flows of profits, interest and dividends appear in this part of the accounts: new loans or investments appear in the third section. Government current

*Table 19*

*United Kingdom: Balance of Payments 1974*
*(£ million)*

| | | |
|---|---|---|
| 1 | *Visible trade* | |
| | Exports | 15 589 |
| | Imports | 20 848 |
| | Balance of Trade | −5 259 |
| 2 | *Invisible trade* | |
| | Private services (net) | +1 073 |
| | Interest, profit, dividends (net) | +1 247 |
| | Government current expenditure abroad (net) | −889 |
| | Invisible balance | +1 431 |
| | *Balance of Trade* plus *invisible balance* equals *Current balance* | −3 828 |
| 3 | *Investment and capital flows* | |
| | Overseas investment in UK | +2 615 |
| | UK investment overseas | −1 375 |
| | Short term private capital flows | +951 |
| | Total investment and capital flows | +2 191 |
| 4 | *Balance item* | +1 147 |
| | *Current balance* plus *investments and capital flows* plus *balancing item* equals: *Total Currency Flow* | −565 |
| 5 | *Official financing* | |
| | Borrowing by HM Government | +644 |
| | Additions to (−) official resources | −79 |
| | | +565 |

*Source: Economic Trends 1975*

expenditure largely takes the form of the maintenance of bases and embassies abroad.

In 1974 the surplus on invisible trade was not enough to offset the deficit on visible trade, there being a net deficit of £3828. This combined deficit (or surplus) is termed the Balance of Payments on current account or, more briefly, the current balance.

The rest of the accounts are concerned with capital flows. The third part of the Balance of Payments records capital flows other than those with which the government is officially concerned. New foreign investments made by United Kingdom companies or banks appear as an outflow and vice versa. These investments can be either direct (the acquisition of physical assets), or portfolio investments (the acquisition of shares and securities). The other item in our summary is the net flow of short-term capital, such as money deposited in (or withdrawn from) a United Kingdom bank by an overseas resident. Although the transactions in this part of the account do not directly involve the United Kingdom government there is some official involvement. Thus ministers have spent time persuading various Arab governments to hold some of their reserves in Sterling in London. This currency was not lent to the government directly and hence the transaction does not appear under official financing.

The sum of the current balance, the net flow of investment and capital and the fairly large balance item (due to under-recording of some transactions) gives the net currency flow. This is really the bill that the government has to pick up. It finances the net currency flow in one of two ways: it either borrows directly from other governments or international monetary institutions, or it allows the stock of gold and foreign exchange to decline. In 1974 the government borrowed £644m, rather more than the amount needed, and hence added £79m to the reserves. The addition appears as a negative (by convention) in the accounts, thus ensuring that the total of official financing is just equal and opposite in sign to the net currency flow. The Balance of Payments therefore balances.

We have explained the accounts with reference to the United Kingdom 1974 position but obviously the balance of each of the five sections can take on any sign—the only constraint is that the accounts in total must balance out to zero.

## Exchange rates

A modest Balance of Payments surplus on current account is one of the policy targets of most governments. Although it is clearly not possible for them all simultaneously to achieve this target it remains their objective. In practice most countries are happy with modest deficits on current account as long as they are not accompanied by capital outflows. The problems arise when persistent and substantial deficits occur as these become increasingly difficult to finance. A deficit on current account can be offset by net inflows of private capital but these are not likely to occur in the face of serious imbalances in the current account, as the latter may lead to expectations of exchange rate depreciations. Thus at the end of the day the government has to finance the deficit either, as we have seen, by borrowing or by running down its foreign exchange reserves. This can only go on for so long. The analogy often drawn between a country with a deficit and a household which is spending more than it earns is a useful one here. A household can do this by running down its assets or by borrowing, but for most households there are limits to their ability to do this. So it is with countries. Most countries' holdings of reserves are small compared with, say, their level of imports and there are limits to their ability to borrow from others.

Some method has to be found of bringing the Balance of Payments back into equilibrium. This normally, but not always, means improving the current balance. One adjustment mechanism is the exchange rate.

The *exchange rate* is the rate at which one currency can be traded for another on foreign exchange markets. Since 1972, with some important exceptions, the exchange rate of most countries has been largely determined by the demand for, and supply of, that currency. Prior to 1972, virtually every country fixed the rate at which its currency could be converted into others but this system has now largely ended.

If we view the exchange rate as the price of a currency, then like any other price that is market-determined it will tend to fall if supply exceeds demand and vice versa. As our example let us take the case of Sterling and, for simplicity, let us take German Marks as representing all other currencies. Thus on foreign exchange markets a demand for Sterling will constitute a supply of Marks and vice versa. Let us look at the sources of the supply and demand for Sterling, linking these up with the Balance of Payments accounts.

One source of demand for Sterling will come from UK exporters. They will be paid in Marks (foreign currency) and will pay these into their bank accounts. The banks will then sell Marks and buy Sterling in the foreign exchange markets. Imports will constitute a supply of Sterling as importers instruct their banks to acquire Marks to purchase imports. Thus we can see that, other things being equal, a visible trade deficit (imports greater than exports) will lead to an excess supply of Sterling at current exchange rates and hence the rate of exchange of Sterling will fall—fewer Marks will be obtainable per unit of Sterling.

The items on the invisible balance can be treated in the same way. Imports and exports of services will lead to corresponding supplies of, and demands for Sterling, respectively, in foreign exchange markets. Similarly receipts of profits, interest and dividends will give rise to demands for Sterling (supplies of Marks) as the UK recipients deposit the Marks at their banks, and vice versa.

We can thus see that if the United Kingdom Balance of Payments on current account is in deficit then, ignoring capital flows for the moment, the exchange rate will tend to fall and if the current account is in surplus the exchange rate of Sterling will rise.

These changes in the exchange rate, which are determined by the state of the current account, will now in turn start to affect the current account itself. To show this we take the case where the UK current account is in deficit: the resulting excess supply of Sterling causes the exchange rate to fall from say £1 = DM6 to £1 = DM5. This alters the relative price of UK and German (foreign) goods both in the UK and abroad. A UK export with a price of £100 will now cost DM500 as opposed to DM600 previously. Thus the quantity of UK goods demanded abroad will tend to rise. The Sterling price of imports, on the other hand, will rise. A good which a German exporter is selling at DM600 will rise in price in the UK from £100 to £120. Thus the quantity of imports will tend to fall.

The effect of the exchange rate change on the UK Balance of Payments on current account will depend upon the elasticity of UK demand for imports and the German elasticity of demand for UK exports. The greater are these elasticities, the greater will be the improvement in the current balance. We can see intuitively why this is so. In the case of UK exports, the more elastic is German demand, the greater will be the quantitative response to the decline in price, and hence the greater the amount of revenue from exports. Similarly the greater the elasticity of demand for imports, the greater will be the decline in import volume as a result of the increase in the Sterling price of imports. If the import and export elasticities were very low it is possible that a decline in the exchange rate would *worsen* the current balance. That is, the import volume and the export volume would each change very little and as import and export prices would be higher and lower respectively, the balance of export receipts and import expenditures would change adversely. It is possible to prove that the limiting case, where a change in the exchange rate leaves the current balance unchanged, is where the import and export demand elasticities sum to unity. For a significant improvement in the balance the elasticities need to add up to something more—say 2 or 3.

Even where the elasticities are of the right order of magnitude, there is a problem of timing. We have treated importers and exporters as reacting immediately and simultaneously to the change in prices, but this is rarely possible. It takes time for demand and supply to adjust to price changes. This has given rise, at least in the UK, to what is known as the J-curve (see Figure 11).

What happens is roughly as follows. Following a depreciation in the exchange rate the Sterling prices of many imports are marked up quickly although the prices of manufactured imports tend to rise after a lag as price lists and catalogues have to be changed. The elasticity of demand for the imports as a group in the UK is less than unity in the short run. Thus the proportionate fall in demand is less than the proportionate rise in price and the import bill (in Sterling) rises fairly quickly. On the export side the immediate effect is not symmetrical. There will be some lags in the response of price lists but more importantly the supply of exports has to be increased and, to be

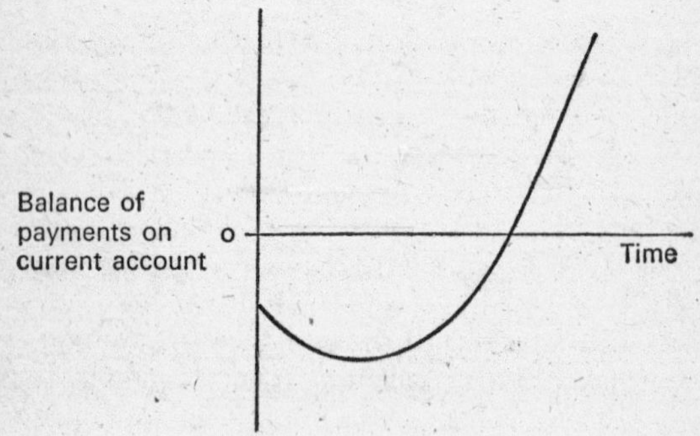


*Figure 11: The J-curve*

successful, the price reductions have to be accompanied by sales and marketing efforts by UK exporters. The volume of exports will respond slowly to the price change. Hence the short-run effect is to worsen the Balance of Payments as import payments rise and export receipts rise slowly. As time proceeds the Balance of Payments slowly improves as the export response increases until it moves into surplus and eventually to rough balance.

Now we need to look at this whole process more carefully. The first point to emphasise is that, to be effective, significant changes in the exchange rate have to be accompanied by demand management policies. To show this let us repeat the equation we introduced in Chapter 2.

$$Y = C + I + G + (X - M)$$

This was the equilibrium condition for aggregate output; national output ($Y$) had to be just equal to the amount of aggregate demand which comprised consumption ($C$), investment ($I$), government expenditure on goods and services ($G$) and the balance of imports and exports of goods and services ($X - M$).

Now we re-write this as:

$$(X - M) = Y - (C + I + G)$$

We started our example with a trade deficit. Thus $(X - M)$ was negative, implying the sum of consumption, investment and government expenditure on goods and services was greater than current output. The exchange rate will tend to improve the trade balance and hence increase the value of $(X - M)$ turning it from negative to more or less zero. It is obvious from the second equation that this will only be possible if, given the value of aggregate output, the sum of the domestic expenditure is reduced. This will happen to some extent as a result of the relative price changes induced by the depreciation but this is not likely to bring about the required quick shift of resources out of production for domestic demands and into the production of exports and import substitutes. Thus large exchange rate changes—and particularly the devaluations that occur under a fixed exchange rate régime—need to be accompanied by a reduction in aggregate domestic demand brought about by the sort of policies discussed in Chapter 4. It is probable that the long lag between the 14% devaluation of Sterling in 1967 and any appreciable improvement in the current balance was largely due to insufficient reductions in aggregate domestic demand. If the process starts with slack in the economy, then there is no need for aggregate domestic demand to be reduced following a depreciation of the currency. This situation is called *export-led growth* and is supposed to be very virtuous.

A second complication that we should take note of stems

from the J-curve. The Balance of Payments worsens immediately following the depreciation and therefore in foreign exchange markets there will be an excess supply of Sterling even at the new, lower, exchange rate. The exchange rate will tend to decline further and so the process might go on. Eventually, however, the full effects of the first depreciation will come through and this will cause a reversal of the secondary depreciations. The problem is that some resources will have switched into the production of exports and import substitutes as a result of the secondary depreciations, and these will now have to move back. This will involve costs. All of this could be avoided if the exchange rate had been prevented from declining further.

If we assume that the initial depreciation was adequate, given time, to bring the current balance into equilibrium then people and institutions who are well informed of this will have the opportunity of making a speculative profit. There are various ways of doing this but, if we remember that the value of Sterling will tend to decline and then increase, to show a profit speculators will have to buy as Sterling depreciates to sell again when it recovers. In doing this they will reduce the extent to which Sterling depreciates initially and will reduce the amplitude of the fluctuations in the exchange rate. This is known as *stabilising speculation* and it is a matter of some importance and of debate whether speculation *is* of this sort, or whether it *de*stabilises the exchange rate.

Another possibility is that the government can act to stabilise the rate by buying Sterling on the down-swing of the J-curve. This is preferable if one believes that governments are better informed than speculators.

Our discussion of government intervention and speculation introduces two final points to be discussed in this section. The present international financial system is not one of freely fluctuating exchange rates, solely determined by market forces, but is best described as 'managed floating'. That is, major participants in exchange markets are governments or, more correctly, Central Banks. Central Banks hold a country's foreign exchange reserves and can use these to influence the rate of exchange. If, in our example, the UK government wished to support the exchange rate of Sterling in the face of downward pressure on the rate, it can sell Marks and buy Sterling. This method was the one used before 1972 when the UK, like most other countries, had a fixed exchange rate. When the rate was fixed between £1 = $2.38 and £1 = $2.42, the only way the Bank of England could enforce this rate was to stand ready to sell Sterling and buy foreign currency if the rate threatened to move outside the upper limit (which did not happen very often), and to buy Sterling and sell foreign currency from the reserves when the rate threatened to fall below $2.38. Under the present system of managed floating there is no fixed rate to support, and governments intervene mostly to even out short-term fluctuations in the rate.

Finally a word or two more on speculators, who may be seen as the 'good guys' when they stabilise the exchange rate, but who are more often presented as the villains of the piece. There are very few people who do nothing but speculate in foreign exchange. Those who speculate are importers or exporters, multinational companies, financial institutions and so on, who, from time to time, often as a matter of prudence, take up foreign exchange positions. A common example of a situation where traders speculate would be the case of a UK importer who in six months' time will have to settle in Marks an invoice for German goods. His expectation is that by then the exchange rate of Sterling to Marks will have depreciated. If he waits six months before acquiring Marks then he will have to pay more for them. To avoid this loss he could buy Marks now, and deposit them in a German bank to earn interest for six months.

Alternatively he could buy Marks 'six months forward' in the forward exchange market. This means that he agrees to buy a specified amount of Marks at the forward rate ruling now: whatever the current rate of exchange is in six months time he will only pay the forward rate ruling now. To the extent that the market shares his view of the future then six months forward Marks will cost more than 'spot' Marks, i.e. Marks purchased now. In this second case our trader will keep the money in Sterling in a UK bank for six months. Which of the two courses he follows will thus depend upon the interest rate differential between London and Frankfurt and the forward discount or premium on Marks. In either case he can be said to be speculating against Sterling and if others share his view the result will be downward pressure on the exchange rate, either now or in six months. Another example of speculation would be the exchange decisions of large companies with branches in several countries. These companies will have large amounts of liquid funds which have to be held in one currency or another, and one influence on the decision of how much of each to hold will be expectations of the future course of exchange rates.

We ought, perhaps, to mention 'pure' speculation here, which is defined as selling something you do not possess or buying something with no funds. By definition this can only take place on forward markets. The trick is this: say you sell Francs which you do not possess three months forward because you expect that the spot price in three months time will be less than the current three months forward price. If you are right, then you acquire the Francs in the spot market to fulfil the three month contract and show a turn on the deal. Pure speculation is not confined to foreign exchange markets but can take place wherever there is a forward market or, as in the case of the Stock Exchange, when all transactions that take place in a certain period are settled on one day at the end of the period.

There are times when speculation for or against a currency reaches whirlwind proportions with tens of millions of pounds moving into a certain financial centre each day. Such events have to be treated differently from the more routine activities described above and we deal with speculative flights in the next section.

## International monetary history

Towards the end of the Second World War the allied countries began preparations for setting up international monetary institutions which would avoid a repetition of the monetary instability, 'beggar my neighbour' policies, and heavy unemployment that characterised the 1930s. The aim was to devise a system that would give stability to exchange rates—to reduce the uncertainties of international trade—and which would be compatible with the maintenance of full employment. The plans were settled at a conference held at Bretton Woods in 1944. The British delegate was J. M. Keynes who presented a radical solution which involved the creation of an international money—'bancor'—but inevitably it was the Americans who carried the day. Their delegate was Harry D. White who, ironically, was exposed as a communist in the McCarthy trials. The system agreed at Bretton Woods lasted until 1971.

The principal institution created was the International Monetary Fund, which formally came into being in 1948. The Soviet Bloc did not join the Fund but most other countries did. Each country had to fix its exchange rate, normally in terms of the Dollar, which in turn had a fixed price in terms of gold. Exchange parities could be altered but only when a country's Balance of Payments was in fundamental disequilibrium. Each member was allocated a quota and it paid this quota into the fund—75% in its own currency, 25% in gold or Dollars. The idea was that to tide a country over temporary deficits it could borrow other currencies from the fund. During its first ten years the Fund was largely ineffective due to the overwhelming dominance of the Dollar, because the quotas were too small, and because there was a reluctance to borrow from the Fund. Subsequently the quotas were increased and the resources of the Fund were further strengthened by extra credit made available to the Fund by the 'Group of Ten', the world's ten richest nations.

By the mid-1960s, however, the Bretton Woods system was increasingly coming under strain. The main source of strain was the Dollar. Under a fixed exchange rate system it is necessary, as we have seen, for countries to hold reserves in order, among other things, to intervene in foreign exchange markets to maintain exchange parities. In practice exchange reserves were held either in Dollars, Sterling or gold. As the value of trade increased year by year, the volume of reserves needed to increase, in the same way as the domestic money supply expands, roughly as national income rises. It was not possible to increase the stock of gold in monetary use significantly as the bulk of new production went to industrial use or into hoards. Thus new reserves had to come from Sterling or Dollars, and here we come to the paradox. The only way more Sterling or Dollars can enter circulation is by the UK or the USA running a Balance of Payments deficit or lending on a large scale abroad. But if deficits are run or if lending reaches large proportions, other countries lose confidence and hence are increasingly reluctant to hold the currency in their reserves. This loss of confidence set in long ago as far as Sterling was concerned but it was only in the 1960s that the Dollar—which was anyway by far the most important reserve currency—came under attack. The Dollar was convertible into gold, at $35 a fine ounce, and up to the mid-1960s the gold reserves of the USA were in excess of its Dollar liabilities. As the flow of Dollars pouring into the system became a flood with the United States' increasing military involvement in South-East Asia its liabilities exceeded its gold reserves and some central banks acted outside the spirit of co-operation by changing their Dollar holdings into gold.

With the loss of confidence in the Dollar and Sterling, other currencies became in demand and from time to time there were massive speculative flights into some European currencies, especially the German Mark. On one day in May 1971 $1000 million was converted into Marks in less than an hour, causing German foreign exchange markets to close. All currencies suffered from these flights. Thus on occasions Sterling came under attack, not because of any underlying weakness of the currency, but simply because the Mark was more attractive than any other currency. At that time the world was still operating the Bretton Woods fixed exchange rate régime and to hold exchange parities Central Banks co-operated in the recycling of speculative funds. In essence what happened was that, as other currencies were exchanged by speculators for Marks in Germany, the German authorities then swapped Marks for other currencies. Despite this co-operation exchange rate changes did occur. Sterling was devalued by 14% in 1967 and, following the speculative onslaught in 1971, the Mark was allowed to find its own level in foreign exchange markets, the result being an effective revaluation of about 3%.

In 1971 the United States government ended its commitment, which had existed since before the war, to convert Dollars into gold at $35 an ounce. At the same time the United States made it clear that it desired other currencies to increase in value relative to the Dollar. The United States, unlike other countries, was not able to devalue without the co-operation of all other countries as the parities of all currencies, under Bretton Woods, were fixed in terms of the Dollar. The suspension of the convertibility of the Dollar had so traumatic an effect that foreign exchange markets were closed for a week and, in fact, the major currencies did float against the Dollar. The float was seen as a temporary measure until a realignment of fixed rates could be achieved and at the end of 1971 the industrial countries concluded the so-called Smithsonian agreement.

A new price of gold was set—$38 an ounce—although the convertibility of the Dollar into gold was severely restricted, by agreement. New parities were established—the Yen, Guilder, Mark, and Swiss and Belgian Francs were up-valued by around 10–17%—and the permitted margins either side of parity were widened. The spirit of Bretton Woods remained, however, although the basis of the system was now the Dollar, not gold. The alternative to a system of fixed exchange rates is a system of floating rates where exchange rates are determined by the supply of and demand for each currency.

In teaching economics as late as 1970 one ritually rehearsed the arguments for and against floating rates, but the possibility that they might actually be introduced was not seriously discussed, contravening, as it did, the inbred conservatism of bankers. In 1973, however, the Smithsonian agreement was broken and the United States, the United Kingdom and several European countries decided to float their currencies and the Bretton Woods era ended.

We are now, as we explained earlier, in a world of managed

floats. The odd vestige of fixity remains—for example in the Common Market 'snake', where movements between the parities of a few members are limited—but essentially we have a floating exchange rate régime, legalised in the Jamaica agreement of 1970.

The great advantage of the floating system is that it can accommodate international differences in the rate of productivity growth and the rate of inflation. In 1974–5 the United Kingdom chose to have an inflation rate considerably higher than the average rate ruling in industrial countries and accordingly the rate of exchange depreciated. Similarly, as our rate of productivity growth lags behind that of most other countries, our competitiveness slowly weakens and with it the Balance of Payments. As we have seen, this leads to an excess supply of Sterling, the exchange rate depreciates and this will tend to bring the current account back into equilibrium.

Underlying trends in productivity growth and inflation will remain the main determinants of trends in exchange rates, but flurries of speculative activity will occur from time to time. The important question, to which the answer has not become clear in the short experience of floating rates, is whether speculation may at times become so intensive as to destabilise rates of exchange and to intensify uncertainty in international financial transactions.

FURTHER READING

The material is covered by S. Wells' textbook *International Economics* (Allen and Unwin, 1969).

# 10

# The World Economy

## The different types of economy

There are several major types of economy in the world. One way of ordering them is according to the degree of technological development, with the United States, Canada, Sweden and Switzerland at the top because they have very technologically advanced service, industrial and agricultural sectors, and with Zambia, Lesotho and Nepal at the bottom because the major part of their economies consists of subsistence agriculture of a type that prevailed throughout the world two centuries ago. (This carries with it the idea of economic progress as a movement through the history of technology from 1700 to the present day—a far-reaching definition with interesting implications.) But another method of ordering economies is in terms of the way in which decisions are taken.

Thus, in the OECD countries, dominated quantitatively by the United States, the predominant form of economic decision-making is by private business firms, with consumers making choices between alternative forms of consumption. This, broadly speaking, is the capitalist world. Even in the most extreme 'capitalist' countries, like the United States and Switzerland, the public sector is large, as has been explained. But there are OECD countries, like Sweden and the United Kingdom, where the public sector is so large a proportion of the whole economy, that it might be advisable to regard them as a specific type of economy—the social democratic. The OECD also contains low income countries, like Turkey, which are really variants of a different sort of economy.

This is the 'Third World' type of economy. It is characterised by low incomes per capita, a predominantly rural economy and 'traditional' modes of production and ways of life. These economies vary enormously, of course, in the nature of their societies, the crops they grow and the way that production is actually organised. But what they have in common is low incomes based on a non-modernised agriculture. They include the Indian sub-continent, most of Africa and much of Latin America.

The fourth type of economy is, of course, Communism. There are four main variants—Soviet, Chinese, Yugoslav and satellite. They are linked by an overt adherence to a set of economic theories associated with Marx. This involves a centrally planned economy, not based on profit and consumer choice, but dedicated to the principle of equality based on 'to each according to his needs, from each according to his abilities'. In the Soviet-type economy, which is heavily industrial, the planning is hierarchical, and devolved from central decisions. In China, the system is based largely on village communes. The emphasis is less on output targets for whole sectors of the economy, and more on a perceived need to raise the levels of work and expectations of the population as a whole by changing each individual's personality. In Yugoslavia, by contrast, the emphasis is put more upon co-operative arrangements in the factories, with a fairly large private enterprise sector. Obviously, as the Marxist sector of the world grows, so will its diversity. But what all parts of the Marxist system have in common is a system of thought, a process of distribution with prices and wages fixed by government, and centralised planning.

## International standards of living

The prosperity of the different parts of the world reflects their differing capital endowment (recent by historical standards, partly dating from the early nineteenth century though mainly from the twentieth). It is, therefore, dependent upon their stocks of capital goods, which in turn depend upon the rates at which capital has been accumulated.

In the Third World there is an absolute scarcity of agricultural and industrial capital. Each Indian, for example, has less than one-seventieth of the electrical power to help him in his daily life, both at work and at home, used by the average

Swede, and there is the same sort of contrast between the energy consumption per capita of other 'developed' countries and those of the Third World (Table 20):

*Table 20*

*1973 Consumption per Head in Kg of Coal Equivalent*

| | |
|---|---|
| Nigeria | 67 |
| Bolivia | 214 |
| Thailand | 303 |
| Italy | 2 737 |
| Denmark | 5 547 |
| United States | 11 960 |

*Source: Table 142, United Nations Statistical Year Book 1974*

---

The OECD countries, often colloquially and rather meaninglessly called capitalist countries, are so called, rightly, because *inter alia* their economies have been built around the concept of capital accumulation—'accumulate, accumulate, that is Moses and the prophets' is what Marx said was the first law of capitalism and it is an exact truth. The United States, for example, has half the total Gross National Product of the OECD, as a result of its extremely high rate of capital accumulation between 1850 and 1950.

The Communist world is more diverse. In the USSR the heavy industrial base is extremely capital-intensive, so that its figures for the output of steel, for example, are very large. But the record of the Soviet agricultural sector has been extremely bad. Two major famines have occurred as a result of Soviet rule in the Ukraine, which is one of the most fertile areas of the world. On the other hand, China has achieved great production successes in agriculture compared, not with the agricultural sectors of the OECD economies, but with the achievements of other Asian economies, except Taiwan, Japan and Malaysia. The prosperity of the OECD economies and the degree to which those of the Third World lag behind, are demonstrated in Table 21.

This sort of table shows that there is a hierarchy of standards of living, ranging from the United States, Sweden, Switzerland, Canada and Australia, down through the principal European countries, to the Third World countries which have a standard of living one tenth of that of the richer ones. Does this table reveal anything, either superficially or deeply, which is absolutely true? A moment's thought will show that it does and it doesn't. If you compare an average Swede or American with

*Table 21*

*1971 Average National Income per Head (US$)*

| | |
|---|---|
| Developed countries | 2960 |
| Developing countries | 210 |
| Ethiopia | 75 |
| Indonesia | 109 |
| Pakistan | 170 |
| Egypt | 218 |
| Brazil | 425 |
| UK | 2252 |
| Germany (Federal Republic) | 3182 |
| Canada | 3755 |
| Sweden | 4023 |
| USA | 4580 |

*Source: Table 188, United Nations Statistical Year Book 1974*

an average Indian there are obvious and gross disparities. The Swede will have a house or flat with many conveniences; he will own a car; his children will go to splendid schools; if he is ill he can go to well-trained hospitals; his work is physically light, he has frequent holidays which can range from sailing in the Baltic to visiting the Mediterranean. The Indian will have very little house room; his transport will be a bicycle; his diet will be relatively sparse and monotonous; his medical care will be exiguous; his children's schools will be overcrowded and poor. He will not travel. Above all, he will be surrounded by a sea of unimaginably miserable humanity, whereas in Sweden there are few poor and few immensely rich people.

At an obvious and very important level, then, the comparison of living standards is a true comparison. There can be few Indians who would reject a Swedish standard of living and there can be few Swedes who would accept an Indian standard of living permanently, though they might be prepared to try it for an experiment.

Of course when reasonably similar countries are compared, then the comparisons have a spurious precision if they are expressed numerically. This is for two reasons. First, the rate of exchange that is adopted reflects the relative strength of the currencies on the foreign exchange market, rather than what the two countries' cost of living actually is. In practice this tends to make countries with a strong currency seem richer than they in fact are. The second reason for qualifying comparison is that people give different values to diff things. By and large, for example, the English have more better housing than the French while the French have b food than the English. A comparison weighted in favour of food will show the French to have a higher standard of living than the English, while one weighted in favour of housing will show the English to be better off than the French.

These two points are important. They become of overwhelming significance when two fundamentally different cultures are under discussion. A Hindu, for instance, takes a radically different view of the purpose of life, and of what is the good life, from a typical West European. There are things that are valued by African tribesmen which are almost inconceivable to Europeans and there are things in Europe—customs, habits, services and commodities—that are of no interest to an African. It does not follow that if the per capita income in Africa is \$200 a year while that in a Western European country is \$2000 a year, the difference in the perceived or subjective standard of living is anything like proportionate. Nevertheless, it *is* true that the \$2000 represents the opportunity of doing things and acquiring goods and services that the African might like to have. So in that strictly neutral sense the European is indisputably better off than the African.

## Economic growth

The standard of living, then, is not a simple concept. In fact it is extremely complex when international comparisons are made because the whole way of life of different countries is what is in question. Oddly enough, of course, this applies not only to geographical comparisons, of Zaire with Ireland, say, but to historical comparisons. A Victorian clergyman would not necessarily regard contemporary English life as manifestly superior to the way of life to which he had been accustomed, though we would say that substantial growth had taken place between the two periods. A Victorian coalminer would presumably welcome most changes that occurred; but even then he might have reservations about some things. Thus when we compare growth between different countries, or economic systems, we are talking about the transformation of whole societies, and no transformation is ever wholly for the better; it is bound to have both positive and negative aspects. A new town built to replace a slum, for example, destroys the countryside.

That being said, the concept of growth is not a neutral one; it means, basically, capital accumulation, mainly in industry, and the consequent output of manufactured goods, as well as the transformation of agriculture by the adoption of new techniques and massive increases in output. Measured by these criteria, the rate of growth in Third World economies has been very low; static for many years; and rarely rising at more than 2% annually. In the OECD countries the average annual rate of growth in the period between 1945 and 1975 was between 3% and 5%. But, even then, there are great exceptions. Great Britain and the United States grow usually at a slower rate, while other countries like Germany and France have grown faster. Countries which were industrialising like Japan, Spain and Yugoslavia have had rates of growth between 7% and 10%. In Communist countries the rates of growth have been equally high for the reason that they have been undergoing the transformation into manufacturing countries and they have at the same time maintained extremely high levels of investment.

*Table 22*

*Average Annual Rates of Growth of Real Gross National Product in Selected OECD countries*

| | *1964–74* |
|---|---|
| Canada | 5·4 |
| USA | 4·0 |
| Japan | 9·4 |
| France | 5·4 |
| Germany | 4·4 |
| Italy | 4·7 |
| United Kingdom | 2·7 |
| All OECD countries | 5·0 |

*Source: OECD Economic Outlook*

There is a further point to be mentioned. In all the countries with high rates of growth the transformation of the labour force by substantial efforts in education has proved to be a crucial factor in the long run.

## Causes of economic growth

Different rates of economic growth then, depend primarily upon the level of investment in manufacturing industry, together with the alteration of the industrial skills of the labour force, which in turn is dependent upon the level of education—both formal and informal. To this must be added certain other elements of great importance. The growth of manufacturing depends upon the use of substantial amounts of labour; much of this labour arises from a high birth rate, or from high levels of immigration, as in North America and Australasia, but in the older countries chiefly from the release of substantial numbers from subsistence agriculture. Thus, historically, the industrial revolution in Britain was preceded by the agricultural revolution. This precedence was necessary both to provide the food for the industrial workers to eat, and to provide the workers for the factories.

To this must be added the transformation of technology. It might seem that a machine is a machine is a machine, and that its output would be the same everywhere. Yet this is not so; the productivity of a unit of investment is high in a high productivity economy and low in a low productivity economy. Thus the adoption of new technology, whether imported, or developed at home, is a complex matter since it depends not only on how many new machines are built, but on the technological environment in which they are developed. This creation of a technologically oriented economy is of basic importance to the question of growth.

To this must be added the ability to sell the goods that technology produces. Marx argued that the function of capitalism was to create capital goods. It would then prove impossible to sell them, as the workers earned so little, so a revolution would be necessary to create a society able to consume the goods that could be produced. In fact this was not true. Capitalism proved able to consume what it produced. This was partly because of population growth, partly because of rising incomes; but above all, because of trade. In most capitalist economies the export trade played a vital part in the expansion of certain key industries. This process is still not fully understood, but it is clear that the growth of world trade plays a vital part in economic growth in the non-Communist countries. In the Communist countries a similar role is played by the central plan which enjoins fast growth in the basic heavy industries. In the agricultural and consumer goods sectors of the economy the Communist nations have not succeeded in achieving high rates of growth, apart from the once-for-all transformation of Chinese agriculture.

## The Third World

The central problem of the highly diverse Third World remains. From the Andes, to the Congo, to the Ganges, there are over 1 billion people living for the most part in dire poverty. Their societies vary a great deal, and their economic situation varies too. Some are in hot climates, and others in cold, some near the sea and others deep inland. What links them is their desperately low level of income per head.

They are characterised by high birth rates. In the past three generations their death rates have fallen, partly as some of the more gross diseases have been moderated, and partly as levels of food output have risen. The phenomenal growth of population which has resulted from these high birth rates and falling death rates has meant that such growth of output as there has been has mostly been absorbed by the growing population, so that the standard of living has barely risen. In parts of India and Bangladesh it has fallen. The exceptions to this have been countries like Singapore and Taiwan, where massive industrialisation has occurred, or countries like Malaysia and Ghana where the agricultural sector has been transformed, chiefly by plantation agriculture. In the oil-rich countries, too, the level of incomc is high (though it is extremely unequally distributed), but there the population is for the most part sparse.

The question that arises is whether or not the economic condition of the Third World can be transformed. In the past two generations changes have occurred. Certain countries and regions have made progress, while others, notably India, seem to have made little. Substantial amounts of overseas investment have been undertaken, but this investment has for the most part been into oil, minerals and plantation agriculture.

It is unclear whether this investment and the subsequent large export flows it generates cause economic development or not. According to Marxists, the investment is purely exploitative. The investment goes in; the copper comes out; and nothing is left. Yet ordinary observation and economic theory suggest that it is not as simple as that. The investment has a considerable effect on the local economy; the development of mineral resources and above all of agriculture requires large quantities of local labour, and the result is the dramatic modernisation of a sector of the economy. Whether or not this modernisation spreads to other sectors is a complex matter which depends very much upon the social structures of the country concerned. In Malaysia and Singapore, for example, the economic development of parts of the economy has affected the whole economy. Yet in nineteenth-century Ireland, Belfast and its hinterland remained an enclave, not affecting the rest of rural Ireland very much.

The nature of these barriers is subject to much anthropological and sociological analysis. It is evident that in many cases they are very deep, which calls the role and likely effectiveness of overseas aid very much into question. Overseas aid has taken

*Table 23*

*Aid from Developed Market Economies*
*(US $ million)*

| | *1969* | *1970* | *1971* | *1972* |
|---|---|---|---|---|
| Direct aid | 5369 | 5583 | 6257 | 6527 |
| Via multilateral institutions (UN agencies, World Bank Group etc) | 1060 | 1137 | 1354 | 1919 |
| **Total** | **6429** | **6720** | **7610** | **8446** |

*Source: Table 192, United Nations Statistical Year Book 1973*

place on a substantial scale, though the developing countries and the aid agencies believe it to be too low.

Figures for 'official development assistance' from developed market economies to the developing countries are shown in Table 23.

The average amount of aid received from these sources is shown in Table 24.

The aid has, however, been singularly unsuccessful in raising income levels except in countries whose growth would probably have taken place anyway. Success in this field, as in others, feeds on success. The aid story, according to Gunnar Myrdal, the greatest and wisest authority on the subject, is the story of the resistance of traditional societies which have deeply corrupt political élites. According to him, and to those who respect the achievements of China, the necessity is for a radical transformation of traditional society, by the use of mass conversion and the example of heroic and dedicated figures. Gandhi, had he lived, might have been as successful as Chairman Mao in revolutionising agriculture.

There are two critical issues which have to be raised. One is the question of the size and growth of population. According to Mao, the huge Chinese population is an asset. Yet the bulk of experts on development would regard birth control as a necessary preliminary to any effective growth. But not only does birth control require a degree of knowledge and education, particularly among village women, it also requires an incentive. In a rural area, the more mouths in a family, the more hands to work the land. And the more babies, the more likely are the parents to have somebody to look after them when they are old. So the whole structure of rural society has to alter before population control becomes either feasible or desirable.

*Table 24*

| *Region* | *Country* | *Total US $ (million)* | *Total per head (US $)* |
|---|---|---|---|
| Africa | Algeria | 113 | 7·34 |
| | Ethiopia | 53 | 2·06 |
| | Nigeria | 88 | 1·51 |
| America | Brazil | 92·1 | 0·93 |
| | Guyana | 12·1 | 16·11 |
| | Surinam | 30·7 | 72·98 |
| Asia | India | 793 | 1·41 |
| | Philippines | 151 | 3·87 |

*Source: Table 202, United Nations Statistical Year Book 1974*

The pressure of population depends partly on the availability of land. In Asia land is scarce. In large parts of Africa it is abundant. It follows, then, that the question of population is also tied up with the land question. This is a further reason for believing that a prior condition to a population policy is attention to other matters.

It has already been said that the twin purpose of altering the mode of agricultural production is to increase output, of food especially, and also to release labour to work in the industrial sector. It is a necessary fact that, as world output per head grows, an increasing proportion of it must be in manufactured goods, since the demand for food grows more slowly than the capacity to produce goods and services. It follows, then, that if there is growth in the world economy taken as a whole, the agricultural sector must grow more slowly than the non-agricultural sector. The big issue for many countries is whether this shift should take place within their own economy, or internationally. For example, New Zealand and Denmark could sustain a high standard of living by producing far more food and raw materials than they could possibly require, while the United Kingdom imported food and raw materials and exported manufactures. This is the classic nineteenth-century division of labour. But increasingly such countries feel the need to become relatively self-sufficient in manufacture, because it lessens their dependence on overseas suppliers (which is the mirror image of the European drive to self-sufficiency in food supplies) and because the output per head in manufacture seems higher than that in agriculture.

In developing nations, which are primarily rural economies, the major question is whether to industrialise or not. Some industrial development is of course both inevitable and necessary. There have to be small factories to service agriculture; there has to be electricity, and small consumer goods industries. But, beyond that, is it desirable for every country to have steel and shipbuilding industries, to manufacture cars and tractors and tanks?

It used to be said that every newly independent Third World country had to have its own flag and its own airline. To this has now been added its own military dictatorship and, as Gavin Kennedy has shown, the need to produce some military goods locally is now a strategic necessity. Similarly, as a matter of patriotism, countries wish to be independent of overseas suppliers for major industrial goods. This is not necessarily true of the smaller countries, but it is true of countries like India and Pakistan, Iran and Egypt.

One of the major components of growth is the desire for 'modernisation', the desire to be part of the modern world. That means electricity, steel and machinery.

The book ends, then, where it began. It was said that originally economics was the study of the wealth of nations. In studying the developing nations of the Third World, the material being studied is the poverty of nations. What is it that has enabled countries like those of Western Europe and North America to 'take off' into sustained economic growth, while old civilisations like those of India and Bengal, or tribal civilisations like those of Africa have not successfully caught the infection of modernity. It may be because they reject (from their own strength) the dissolution of social institutions that accompanies the process of economic change, because their own social institutions are so strong. Or it may be that their social institutions are so weak that they are unable to sustain the process of continuous economic development, with all the robust and vigorous endeavours that are necessary if it is to be effective.

The major questions of economics, then, such as why are the poor countries poor, depend for their ultimate answers on a breadth of knowledge that goes far beyond economics.

FURTHER READING

The classic analysis of the problem of underdevelopment is Myrdal's massive work, *Asian Drama* (Penguin, 1968); see also the same author's *The Challenge of World Poverty* (Penguin, 1971).

# Index